PLAY DIRECTION
A Practical Viewpoint

PLAY DIRECTION
A Practical Viewpoint

John Counsell

David & Charles : Newton Abbot

0 7153 6261 5

Set in 11 on 13 pt Pilgrim
and printed in Great Britain
by Clarke Doble and Brendon Limited Plymouth
for David & Charles (Holdings) Limited
South Devon House Newton Abbot Devon

For JOAN RILEY

with admiration and gratitude

CONTENTS

ILLUSTRATIONS

FOREWORD

by SIR BERNARD MILES, CBE

Founder and Director of The Mermaid Theatre, London

I was apprenticed to John Counsell, so you can imagine the pleasure it gives me to write a tiny foreword to his book. Let me tell you how this happened.

At the end of my final year at Oxford, a friend introduced me to actor/manager Maurice Colbourne, who was setting up a company to tour Canada with a repertoire of Shaw plays. I duly met Maurice and having assured him that I would be happy to be launched in the humblest of capacities, was invited to join the company as Assistant Stage Manager and understudy. Even the very modest salary (I forget the amount) was settled and I was, of course, over the moon with pleasure. 'There is only one little formality,' said Maurice, 'I shall have to show you to my Stage Director, John Counsell, and get his approval. But I don't think you need worry. I'll get him to give you a ring and fix a time to see you.'

So there I was, as I thought, all set to make a resounding debut in the great open spaces of Canada. I telephoned the good news to family and friends and, of course, it soon got around college. But I was not to jump the first hurdle quite so easily.

About a week later the college porter put his head round the door of the Junior Common Room and told me I was wanted on the telephone in the college lodge. 'It's a Mr Counsell,' he said. 'Ah,' thought I, 'this is it! This is where we tie up the ends.' I hurried to the 'phone and it was indeed John at the other end of the line.

After the briefest of introductions he took the plunge. 'I'm afraid I have a disappointment for you, old boy. Our leading lady has just got married and she has asked if he can join the company. Naturally, Maurice doesn't want to part the newly-weds so soon, especially for a long trip like this, but we can't afford to take him without dropping you. It's a tight squeeze financially as it is. Maurice will be writing to you but I thought I had better let you know right away. I'm awfully sorry.'

So my early hopes were dashed and the British theatre had to wait a whole year for my debut. I spent that year happily enough teaching English, History, Mathematics and Rugby football at Southcliffe School, Filey. But when the call came again it came once more from John, who was now helping Baliol Holloway to put together a production of *Richard III* at the New Theatre. When they reached the point of choosing the ASMs and understudies and Holloway asked John if he had any ideas, John turned up trumps. 'Well, I do know a chap who might be useful,' he said. 'He hasn't done anything yet but he's intelligent and he's quite handy with tools and a paintbrush so he can make himself useful.' This useful chap was yours truly and I was duly signed up at £4 a week to act as one of John's ASMs and to play a pall-bearer and the second messenger and to understudy seven small parts. I also received an extra pound a week for painting props and shields under the guidance of one of London's great property masters, Harry Langham.

Holloway's fine *Richard* folded up after a very brief run and after a stint as scene painter at the Fortune, I went off on a twenty-week tour of *St Joan* with Lewis and Sybil Casson, once more for £4 a week; lived handsomely in theatrical bed-sitting rooms for £2 10s a week all-in and came home with £15 in the Post Office Savings Bank. After a month or two spent packing chrysanthemums and gladioli on my father's nursery, John called me to the colours once more. The date was now 1933 and he had become infected with the bug of management, the vision of wielding power from the top office, and the pitch he had chosen was Windsor. There I joined him as resident designer and scene painter, and there I spent one of the happiest years of my life under his tutelage, not only designing and painting the sets but acting small parts and making myself generally useful. I even designed the letterhead used on Theatre Royal notepaper for nearly thirty years, a tiny picture of a castle tower standing amid burgeoning trees; and it was at Windsor that the ambition one day to go into management myself (and who knows, perhaps build my own theatre?) first began to sprout.

So you see John was willy-nilly one of the landmarks in my own long and busy professional life and besides the basic ABC of the profession he taught me that the theatre calls for dauntless courage, unending hard work, endless stores of invention and imagination and a high sense of leadership.

Now, after nearly forty years of management and many years practice as a director, he does me the compliment of asking me to write a foreword to this book, the fruit of his long and varied experience. It is neither a big book nor a fussy one and it puts forward no pet theories. It presents the simple basic rules and guide-lines which underlie all theatrical production, indicates many pitfalls to be avoided and offers many wise suggestions drawn from a lifetime in the theatre.

PREFACE

Producing a play, like acting, depends for its success partly on acquired technique but largely upon the personal attributes of the director concerned. What he does by instinct—the prompting of his subconscious mind—will not only give his production individuality but add to the storehouse of his knowledge. Thus, with experience, he builds up his own technique—his own way of doing things.

However, in the early stages, the novitiate director seeking guidance in a field of activity which by its nature has few set rules, must rely upon the experience of others from which to derive whatever ideas and precepts seem most appropriate to his own way of thinking; a starting point from which to begin to work out his own sense of direction. I hope that this book may prove of value as an addition to the stockpile upon which he can draw. It is written strictly from my personal viewpoint, the outcome of producing and directing plays both at my own theatre at Windsor and in London over a period of forty years.

I count myself lucky in having gained my early experience as a director in the hurly-burly of weekly rep. Forty-odd plays of every conceivable kind were produced each year with companies made up of actors at various stages of development, from the raw beginner to the old stager who knew every trick. I, like the actors, had to try my hand at everything, whether or not it seemed to be within my scope. With ridiculously limited rehearsal time and a shoe-string budget, the results were, to say the least, patchy, but the sheer volume of it provided a most valuable clinical experience in learning about plays, the handling of actors and technicians and sorting out one's own capabilities and limitations as a director. As time went on and circumstances allowed for adequate rehearsal time and a more liberal budget, the lessons learnt and the ideas and methods acquired were applied more expansively or, where necessary, were modified. Thus everything written in this book derives from and has been tested by experience.

That experience has however been confined to working in theatres with a proscenium arch. For this reason, I have made no attempt to discuss the special techniques in movement, lighting and decor required in theatres in the round and those with thrust stages. Rather than regurgitate what has already been most admirably written by those who know about them at first hand, I suggest that the aspiring director should seek guidance from the books on the subject listed in the bibliography on page 131.

I am conscious of having failed to overcome the problem posed for anyone writing about the theatre by the lack of any satisfactory generic word which brackets actors and actresses. 'Artist' is I suppose an adequate label for sticking on stage doors or heading salary lists, but is too all-embracing and imprecise in the context of any discussion of the job of acting. A similar nuisance is that there is no possessive pronoun common to both sexes. To refer all the time to 'actors and actresses' and 'he and she' is cumbersome. I have therefore risked the wrath of the ladies by using 'actor' and 'he' throughout with the intention that the words should refer to both sexes.

I have to thank Jonathan Goodman, not only for urging me to write this book but for his advice and criticism throughout all stages of its gestation; Sir Bernard Miles for writing the foreword; Frederick Bentham and B. Bear, of Rank Strand Electric, for vetting the chapter on lighting; my secretary Frankie Godliman for turning my nearly illegible scrawl into beautifully typed script; Richard Berry for the drawings and designs; and Angela Fox and members of my family for their comments and general encouragement.

CHAPTER ONE

Attributes of a Director

Until comparatively recently in the English theatre the words 'producer' and 'director' were synonymous, with the former most frequently used. However, in the American theatre and in films and television, 'producer' and 'director' are two different people with two distinct functions, and as the two latter media increasingly became the chief sources of income for professional artists, it became expedient for the theatre to avoid confusion by following suit.

In broad terms it is the 'producer' who decides to do the play, finds the money, appoints the director and, in consultation with him and usually the author, engages the actors, the designer and other technicians. He provides the organisational structure through which sets, costumes and props are ordered, the rehearsal rooms and theatres are booked and the finances of the enterprise controlled. He will discuss with the director the general lines upon which the play is to be produced and, in the rare event of there being any fundamental disagreement between them, sack the director and appoint another. From the moment rehearsals begin he will, if he is wise, leave everything except strictly business matters to the director and only intervene if asked to do so for some specific purpose.

The French term for director is *metteur en scène* and that in a nutshell describes the physical side of his job. It does not, however, indicate how he prepares what he 'puts on stage' and in this respect the English word 'director' is more helpful. By 'directing' and co-ordinating the actors, designer and other experts, he aims to bring to life on the stage, in vocal and visual terms comprehensible and stimulating to an audience, a play conceived by the author and expressed by him in written terms.

In most professional repertory companies and amateur societies, the two functions are not nearly so clear-cut. They may be carried out by the same person or, more often, the producer's responsibilities are undertaken by a committee, an 'administrator' or a combination of the two. The director is usually appointed by the committee to which he is ultimately responsible.

To be successful a director is likely to have certain personal attributes which combine in varying proportions to fit him for his job. Three of them are indispensable.

First, an instinctive ability to see and feel things in dramatic terms: the faculty meant when it is said of anybody 'he is a born actor' or 'he is a born playwright'. Without it, there would be no point whatever in attempting to work in the theatre, either as professional or amateur. Like most instincts, it is not easy to define. Perhaps it is to see in one's mind's eye events or ideas, factual or fictional, described or enacted on a stage in the pattern or shape which will evoke from an audience a heightened response, compared with its reaction to the same events or ideas read out as straightforward narrative. The story of Hamlet, Prince of Denmark in narrative form would be mildly interesting to an audience who had not heard it before. When Shakespeare, a good director and a first-class company of actors combine to tell it in dramatic terms, the same audience, even though they may have seen it a dozen times before, will be enthralled.

An instinct for the dramatic is an essential basis but it is imagination—the second indispensable attribute—which gives full expression to that instinct and which lifts a play off the page and brings it to life on the stage. It illumines all creative work. According to the degree to which a director possesses it, the more inspired or the more hum-drum his contribution to a production will be.

Thirdly, it is imperative that a director should be able to communicate his ideas clearly and intelligibly. There are few things more exasperating to actors and technicians than having to guess at what the director means, guessing wrong and having to start all over again. An articulate director not only stands a much better chance of getting what he wants, but saves a great deal of precious time and commands a much greater respect.

Other attributes, highly desirable, though not indispensable, are an air of authority, patience, tact, understanding and moral courage. The production of a play is a team effort and the director is the leader of that team. It will almost always be found, among professional actors at any rate, that they will automatically defer to the director ex officio, just as a soldier will defer to his commanding officer. It is up to the director, as it is to the CO, to conduct himself so as to win their respect, trust and even affection.

The director is responsible for the production in its progress from the earliest stages to the first performance before an audience, and then throughout its run. On the way, he will be dealing with some minds which are slower than others, and with the doubts and uncertainties of actors struggling to learn their lines and work out the intricacies of their parts, each with his own particular method and at his own pace. He may find himself having to turn down their well-intentioned ideas because they are out of harmony with the production as he conceived it. He may be confronted by a distressed, stubborn or even angry author vehemently disputing the modifications to the original text which he regards as essential; or an inexperienced author profoundly disappointed that the actors show no signs of portraying the characters exactly as he had originally visualised them.

A handful of famous directors have been notorious for the way they rode roughshod over authors, actors, designers and anybody else in sight and after reducing them all to tears and fearful submission, built up on the scene of desolation a superlative production. It is not, however, a method to be recommended and there can surely be no sound argument against creating a climate in which everybody is happy and eager to operate. At the same time, there must never be any doubt as to who is boss—who must have the last word in any argument.

In addition to such personal characteristics, it is essential that a director, even when faced with his very first production, should have some knowledge of stage craft and an idea of the working of an actor's mind. The former can perhaps be picked up to some extent from books and from observation, although it shows great temerity on anybody's part to take charge of a company without having served at least some time in one of the less responsible positions. In recent years there has been a tendency for young graduates, having made some sort of mark in university dramatic societies, to leap into the theatrical arena as self-styled professional directors. Their self-confidence seldom pays off.

They find themselves drifting into peripheral jobs far removed from those their shining hopes had visualised. There have, of course, been startling exceptions: Peter Brook, for example, and Peter Hall.

For the most part, directors emerge from the ranks of either actors or stage management, and during their time in these capacities have acquired a sound knowledge from the sideline of what is expected of a director. They have learnt the jargon, seen productions come to fruition and, by being on the receiving end of directors' instructions, have had the chance to judge them critically. It is most desirable that a director should have been an actor for however brief a time and with whatever lack of success. Unless one has experienced them oneself, it is probably impossible fully to appreciate the problems with which an actor is faced and his ways of solving them. The relationship between director and actor will be discussed at length in a later chapter; suffice it to say here that it is easily the most important factor in a director's job.

It is also desirable, though not absolutely necessary, that a director should also have at least a smattering of knowledge of every department which will be contributing to the eventual outcome of his efforts. If he has had practical experience in all or any of them so much the better. To be able to talk in their own language to the various experts who will, in fact, be carrying out the work, will be of immense help in his relationship with them. It will substantially increase his chances of getting exactly what he wants, it will save precious time, but above all it will assist him in establishing his authority in areas where an understandable urge to make a personal impact at any cost can destroy the balance of the production. The over-elaborate set, the over-emphatic costumes, the sacrifice in the lighting of luminosity for atmosphere are merely indications that the designer, costumier and light expert are all artists in their own spheres, whose exuberance has not been curbed as it should have been by the director. Again, this matter will be dealt with more fully later.

What has been written so far, and for the most part what follows, refers to any director, whatever the circumstances in which he is working and whatever the play he is directing. Nevertheless, his job will vary greatly according to the requirements of each circumstance and the nature of each play. Taking the two extremes, the professional directing a cast of experienced actors will approach his task quite differently from the director of a cast of totally raw amateurs. The first will be striving to draw out of the actors by encouragement, persuasion and stimulation the finest performances of which they are capable and even with luck carry them beyond what they had regarded as their normal capabilities. At the same time, he will be co-ordinating and orchestrating their individual talents towards achieving a balanced and harmonious performance of the play as a whole. But he will not presume to teach them how to act, any more than the conductor of a professional orchestra would concern himself with teaching a violinist how to play. Both director and conductor would take it for granted that the artists working under them knew their job.

The director of the inexperienced group of amateurs must, of course, have his own 'end product' in mind, but it cannot be so ambitious (or he'll despair) and most of his efforts will be spent in coaching his cast in the rudiments of acting. It can be a very rewarding experience. It is, however, not to be assumed that the teacher who can evoke a surprisingly good performance from the most unpromising material is necessarily capable of inspiring great actors to reach the heights.

In the professional theatre nowadays, there is a tendency
for directors, if not exactly to specialise, at least to undertake
only the kind of productions in which they are, by temperament and experience, most likely to shine. From the audience's point of view, at least, this is a good thing. The brilliant
director of a Shakespearian tragedy might well come sadly
to grief if asked to tackle the average who-dunnit. He will
probably be baffled by the absence of any subtlety of characterisation, any significance underlying the flat statement
to move the plot forward. He will probably attempt to try
logic when the disguise of incredibility might be more appropriate, and by overloading the dialogue and structure of the
play with more than it was meant to bear, destroy the
suspense, intrigue and shocks which are the author's sole
purpose. It need hardly be added that the extremely successful director of thrillers might be even more baffled if confronted with the task of producing *King Lear*.

Shakespeare, Restoration comedies, realistic plays, modern
comedies, farces, Pinter puzzle plays and Becket no-plays all
require a different line of approach and treatment, and rare,
if not non-existent, is the director who can produce every
kind with equal success.

CHAPTER TWO

Choosing the Play

To the director who is also producer of a repertory company, responsible for presenting a continuous programme of different plays over a long period, the choosing of those plays is one of his most important and often difficult tasks, upon which the success or failure of the enterprise to a great extent depends.

In any amateur group, even though the final choice may be made by a committee, it is more than probable that the director will be a leading member of it and that his suggestions and opinions will carry more weight than anyone else's. It is important, therefore, for any director to be able to assess the potential merit of a play when still in script form. To some this comes easily and instinctively, to others through experience. It must be said that 'merit' is not an absolute. What to one director may appear rubbish, to another will seem a masterpiece and in his hands may prove to be so.

The impression gained from the first reading is all-important. The director must ask himself: 'Can I see the action and visualise the characters in my mind's eye? Can I hear the characters speaking in my mind's ear?' If so, the play is at least produceable. At this stage too much thought need not be given to its construction and other technical matters. 'Does the subject interest me? Does it spark off any sort of urge inside me to produce it?' If not, it would probably be advisable to consider it no further, because the *realisation* of a play is in many ways a very personal matter. A director should avoid, if it is at all possible, any which does not appeal to him. Otherwise there is a risk that the result may prove unfair to the play and unfair to the director's reputation. This is not to deny that when circumstances compel a director to tackle a play that does not appeal to him—when, for instance, he is solely responsible for a whole succession of plays in a repertory season—he can, if he knows his job, more often than not overcome his prejudices with reasonable success.

Having decided that the play interests him sufficiently to warrant serious consideration, the director should next read it several times with gradually increasing attention to details, visualising it scene by scene, appreciating its merits, but, more important, seeking out any weaknesses and reassuring himself that these are remediable. In particular, he should make sure that the construction is sound, that the action and the argument form a pattern that is dramatically effective. There are no set rules as to what that pattern should be. For instance, the so-called 'well-made play' in which the plot and story-line are of paramount importance and of which Pinero is often quoted as the archetypal exponent, was and still is written to a recognised formula and is usually in three acts. In the first, the nature of the play, its overall setting and the relationships of most of the principal characters are established, and the general direction of the story-line indicated. In the second, the ideas, situations and relationships thus established progress until they reach a climax. In the third, the consequences of that climax are followed through and the story-line rounded off. Thus the play is divided into a clear-cut beginning, middle and end. (The present day preference for one interval does not necessarily break this pattern as each act can be divided into scenes.)

In contrast, many modern playwrights tend to reject any such rigid structure and to concern themselves more with character, mood and theme than story-line. They aim to achieve dramatic development by the accumulation of incidents and revelations of character, not always at first sight related or explained but which together add up to an expression of the author's creative intention. The object is to induce a subjective mental response from the audience, as opposed to the objective reaction to a play structured in narrative form. Sir Noël Coward is quoted as replying to a young actress's praise of his brilliant dialogue: 'Nonsense, anyone can write brilliant dialogue. It's *construction* that makes a good play.' While few would agree with the first statement, even fewer would disagree with the second—especially, one imagines, those dramatists who eschew the well-tried pattern of the conventional three-act play and seek their own method of achieving what is essential to any authentic dramatic work—exposition, development and dénouement (that is, 'unravelling').

Successful play construction may be defined simply as timing and manipulating these elements in the play in relation to each other in such a way as to produce the dramatic effect the author is seeking; in other words, deciding how and at what point in the play each item of information, each idea and its development and fulfilment, should be given to the audience. This structural relationship may be straightforward and easy for the director to assess. It may be highly intricate and require close study of the text before it becomes apparent. If such study fails to find it, the play is not worth proceeding with.

The next matter for scrutiny is the dialogue, and through it the characterisation. Dialogue must seem to reflect the quality of real speech while at the same time being so contrived as to reveal character and situation and to conform to the requirements of the play's construction. Every line of it must contribute to the evolution of the play. As it will be heard only once by the audience, its impression must be immediate or it is valueless. However, 'impression' must not be confused with 'meaning', which may well not be revealed until later in the play.

It must be natural to each character who speaks it. (A simple test of this is, when reading, to mask the names in the margin of the script and see whether the speaker of each speech is identifiable.) It may be required to indicate mood or establish atmosphere. It must have rhythm and timing, which give the play its style and will enable the actors who speak it to put it across to the audience effectively. (Any experienced actor knows that to change a single word of dialogue written by such great stylists as Shakespeare, Shaw or Coward is virtually impossible without impairing the dramatic value of the sentence in which it occurs.) It must have verbal colour and clarity. Good modern dialogue tends to be spare of literary flourishes and to achieve these essentials by the skilful choice and placing of words which are for the most part in every day use. The writing of dialogue which successfully combines all these qualities is no easy matter.

Unlike a novelist, the dramatist is not in a position to keep total control of the creation of his characters. In the performance of the play, and the process leading up to it, the actor will inevitably interpret what the author has written in terms of his own experience, imagination and personal attributes, conditioned to a greater or less extent by the director's influence. What the audience will be watching is the actor's portrayal of the character, which is rarely the same character as that conceived in the author's mind and given expression in the written text. It is, nevertheless, all-important that the director, when reading the text, should reassure himself that every character in the play has sufficient inherent truth, and consistency of conduct and thought expressed in the dialogue to make an individual to whom an actor could give life.

Apart from these basic considerations of construction, dialogue and characterisation, there are qualities particular to certain types of play which are essential to their successful production.

For instance, the purpose of a who-dunnit thriller is to baffle the audience. To do so, the author sets up as many possible solutions as to who did the murder as he—or she—can evolve from the relationship of the various characters to the corpse and the circumstance of the death. In assessing it, the director should be looking for suspense, the shock of the unexpected, reasonable plausibility in an area of total contrivance, and skill in concealing the final dénouement.

With any historical play the test is whether or not it stands up as a play *per se*, without regard to its factual background and without any assumption that the audience will have any prior knowledge of the subject: in particular, whether the characters live as flesh-and-blood beings created in dramatic form and are not mere descriptions culled from patient research of historical records. History seldom conforms to the requirements of dramatic shape. The climaxes tend to come too soon, events usually sprawl over too long a space of time, characters who dramatically need to clash never meet, and so on. The dramatist tends therefore to be torn between accuracy of fact and theatrical effectiveness. For the play to be acceptable, he must without question give the latter priority. He must also avoid over-elaboration and refrain from stuffing in dramatically irrelevant details which, even if historically interesting, weigh down and falsify the dialogue.

Comedy is defined in the dictionary as 'a light and amusing stage play with a happy ending' and as 'that branch of the drama which adopts a humorous or familiar style and depicts laughable characters and incidents'. As a 'category' it thus covers a wide range of plays from slapstick to the elegance and wit of, say, *The School For Scandal*. Even so there are, in varying proportions, certain elements common to every kind of comedy, and the director will be looking out for their skilful deployment. They are products of the author's comic invention and the humorous slant he gives to his characters, their relationships and the situations in which they become involved. Some of the more important are the sudden release of tension; the shock of the unexpected; incongruity, often depending on exaggeration of character or situation; anti-climax; the fulfilment of the audience's expectation or, on the other hand, its confounding; the belittling of dignity; physical discomfiture.

Almost all these elements of comedy depend for their effect upon the previous setting-up or 'planting' of a situation or idea out of which, and often in contrast to which, the moment of laughter arises. To take an example: at the beginning of the second act of Noël Coward's *Hay Fever*, Richard Greatham, the staid diplomat guest of the eccentric Blisses, finds himself involved in a game which breaks up in a family row. He is off-stage when, towards the end of the act, another family row builds up, and at its climax he enters and asks, 'Is this a game?' This gets an enormous laugh and triggers off a scene of total incongruity. Early in the play it has been established that the line 'Is this a game?' occurred in a play in which Judith Bliss had once starred. She now takes her cue and, with her children joining in, plays the scene through, to the complete bewilderment of Richard and their other guests, building in a crescendo of laughter to a hilarious curtain. The humour of the whole scene depends upon the two situations planted earlier in the play.

However good he considers the play, however much he himself is eager to produce it, the director will almost certainly have to consider other points of view before a decision to do so is taken. The first and foremost should be whether or not it is likely to appeal to the particular audience for which it is intended. One says 'should be' because in these days of subsidies, when actors do not always have to 'please to live' to the same extent as in Dr Johnson's day, the likes and dislikes of the potential audience are too often completely ignored. 'To give the public what it wants' has in certain quarters become a term of derision. Such thinking is either intolerably arrogant in its attitude to those whom the theatre exists to serve, or merely perverse for the sake of perversity. It is to be hoped that anyone reading this book will accept that a performance of a play that has no reasonable hope of attracting an audience has no valid purpose, and that no one except a masochist is willingly going to waste time and money on witnessing a play he heartily dislikes. Should he be persuaded or tricked into doing so at the same theatre on too many occasions, he will seek other ways of spending his leisure time. If a large number of others feel the same, attendance figures at that particular theatre will drop precipitately.

It is the director's job in his capacity as producer to do his best to find plays which will attract and please an audience of sufficient size to justify their production. This applies in whatever kind of theatre or group he is operating. If it is the only professional theatre in a wide area, he will be wise to seek a balanced programme of plays which will appeal in turn to different sections of the public. He will aim at sell-outs of popular successes and at least a worthwhile attendance at plays of a more demanding nature. If it is a coterie or experimental theatre he must bear in mind the tastes of his potential audience just as much.

It must be said, however, that neither the director nor anyone else can ever be really sure that a play is going to succeed. One is accustomed to old theatrical managers gloomily shaking their heads and announcing portentously, as if it had never been said before, 'Ah my boy, if any one of us could be sure of what the public wanted, we'd all be millionaires.' Like most clichés, it has a strong element of truth. Often what starts out with all the likelihood and high hopes of being a certain winner turns out a disastrous flop, and the play which was put in as a stop-gap, or over which everyone has despaired at the dress rehearsal, runs for several years. Agatha Christie's two thrillers *The Hollow* and *The Mousetrap* which reached London in quick succession, are of precisely the same kind and are judged by most people to be of about equal merit. The first ran a matter of months, the second decades. Much research by sociological scholars has sought the reason why and so far no satisfactory answer has been found. This horrible warning of the uncertainties of theatrical management should be heeded but obviously not allowed to oppress too much, or no decisions of any kind would ever be made.

Having found a play which he would like to do and which

c

he thinks would attract a reasonably good audience, the director still has other things to consider. Would the play be within the production and financial resources of the management or group presenting it? In other words, would the building of the sets, the making of the costumes and the mounting of it on the stage available be a feasible operation, and would there be sufficient capital available to finance the production at least up to the opening night and, in the case of a professional company, to cover the running expenses for at least two weeks, the period for which salaries have to be guaranteed?

If the answer to all of these points is favourable there remains the question of casting. He must assure himself that actors are available who are capable of performing the parts in the play up to the standard of production he has set himself.

Although his assessment of the play's merits *per se*, of its suitability and practicability for production in prevailing circumstances, must ultimately be matters of his judgement, a director may gain much of value if it has already been produced elsewhere by finding out about its history. Was it a success or a failure? In either case, why? If a success in London or New York, was it because it had a big star or a strong all-round cast? Was it the only play of its kind running at the time? Did it survive bad patches by dint of having a small cast and being relatively cheap to run? Was it authorship that did it? Was it longevity begetting longevity? (The monumentally long run of *The Mousetrap* can be ascribed to affirmative answers to any one or all of the last four questions.) If it was a success in the provinces, was it for any of the above reasons or had it favourable local connotations? Finally—and this is the crucial question—was it the quality of the play itself?

If it was a failure in London or New York, was it because of a weak cast—weak either intrinsically or as regards 'star' appeal? Was it badly directed? Was it produced in an unsuitable theatre—the fate of far too many good plays? Was it produced during a slump or at a bad time of year? Was it killed by some extraneous circumstance—a strike, war, prolonged heatwave? Was it ahead of its time or unfashionable? Did its title prove unattractive? Is there an inherent but not obvious weakness in the play? Is it one of those plays which, in spite of its undoubted merit, repels an audience because of its theme? (There are many such which, by providing marvellous opportunities for director and actors, are traps for the unwary. A notable instance was *The Wooden Dish*, which was concerned with the tragedy of helpless old age.) With a new play, its case-history is unlikely to amount to more than whether or not it has been previously rejected by other managements and, if so, their reasons for rejection. Needless to say, such information is likely to be given by the author or his agent only with the greatest reluctance. However, since the play has not yet been tested by audience reaction, it would in any case amount to no more than one man's judgement against others'.

It may be, of course, that the director is not concerned in any way with the choice of the play but is just handed the script and told to get on with it. Even so, much of the foregoing is still applicable. Many of the questions which should be asked when choosing a play need also to be asked when the director makes a critical appraisal of any play he is about to produce. The answers will reveal its strengths and weaknesses and determine the lines upon which he will proceed.

CHAPTER THREE

Relationship with the Author

The writing of a play is a creative act and, as with all such, to refer to it as the brainchild of its creator very precisely suggests his attitude towards it. Perhaps because he is aware that he can only reach ultimate fulfilment through others, the dramatist is likely to be even more possessive, protective and instinctively resistant to critical argument about his work than other artists. One soon learns as a manager receiving a constant flow of new plays from hopeful authors how easily hurt they can be. In rejecting ninety-nine out of a hundred scripts, it is wise to be both courteous and firm but not to tangle in any discussion as to the reason for rejection except in the most general terms. Otherwise, a long and increasingly acrimonious correspondence may well ensue.

Having made the point that writers of plays as a breed tend to be exceptionally vulnerable, it would be wrong to suggest that all of them have to be treated with kid gloves. The more professional and experienced he is, the more a dramatist is likely to keep a tight rein on his paternal instinct, recognise and accept that the ultimate realisation of his play will inevitably differ from his conception of it, and be eager to co-operate wholeheartedly in the process of mutation.

A happy relationship between author and director based upon mutual respect for each other's ability is of immense help in achieving the full potential of a play. If it does not come easily it is well worth working on—especially by the director, who in the all-important early stages will almost certainly be at a disadvantage. Whereas he has probably only had the opportunity to read the script a few times, the author has not only written it but lived with it for months or even years and will have a reason, good or bad, for everything. In an early round of argument he is, therefore, likely to come out on top. To avoid this situation, which could lead to mutual mistrust instead of confidence, the director of a new play should regard his first conference with an author, particularly one with whom he has not worked before, as a kind of reconnaissance, upon the outcome of which he can base further strategy. His approach should be one of query rather than comment (except, of course, in generally favourable terms!), inducing the author to do most of the talking. By this means he will discover the general line of the author's thinking, receive clarification of any obscurities in the text, and start gently prodding at the areas where he senses he may subsequently require major changes. He will also be able to assess how sensitive the author is to criticism and how far he is prepared to co-operate.

At the next meeting, the director should do most of the talking, explaining in outline his production intentions, discussing the set and the casting. It is in the context of this overall exposition, on which the author must feel free to comment and to criticise, that the director should bring up and, if necessary, press for any major changes in the text. It is most desirable that as many controversial matters as possible are settled and an agreed script achieved by the time rehearsals begin.

Should the author be one who regards the text he has written as holy writ and who obstinately refuses to make any alterations after reason, persuasion, pleading and cajolery have all been vainly tried in turn, it may be necessary as a last resort for the director to have a blazing row to get what he wants if he considers the issue important enough. During this the author will almost certainly invoke the clause in his contract by which 'Nothing in the text shall be changed without the author's consent', which apparent ace the director will promptly and triumphantly trump with the rest of the clause: 'such consent not to be unreasonably withheld'.

Who in a matter of this kind is to decide what is reasonable and what is unreasonable? Possibly the author's agent and the producer (if he is other than the director) may be called in by their respective sides to thrash the matter out. Should the final decision be in the director's favour, it can, of course, turn out that the author is incapable of writing two new lines of dialogue in less than six months, and this may well be why he dug in his toes in the first place. And the row will start all over again as to who is going to re-write. Fortunately, this sort of situation is the exception rather than the rule.

Another 'Consent not to be unreasonably withheld' clause occurs in most authors' contracts with regard to casting. It is designed to give the author some say, however muted, in a matter which may fundamentally affect the fate of his play. In London and New York, and indeed elsewhere, the casting is frequently distorted by the supposed need for 'names' to ensure a run or even to obtain a theatre. This is likely to be just as objectionable to the director as to the author, especially if the star is not only wrong for the part and may therefore well throw the entire production out of balance, but is unlikely to bring an extra twopence to the box office. (The number of stars who can fill a theatre in England or the United States, regardless of the merit of the play or the quality of their performance in it, can be counted on one hand.) Both director and author will, however, almost certainly have to bow to the demands of the play's promoters, as a *sine qua non* of production. Obviously, when an actor is both a 'name' and right for the part, any refusal of consent by the author would be regarded as totally unreasonable.

When star names are not involved or when supporting characters are being cast, it is seldom that the author and director will disagree to the point of insistence on either side. If the director suggests someone of whom the author disapproves, he will in all probability put forward the next name on his list. Very often casting, particularly of men, is decided not by agreement but by the availability of actors. Although the theatrical profession has outstandingly high unemployment figures, producers and directors seeking to cast plays with actors of talent find that those they want are remarkably often in work.

The attitude that authors are a pestilential nuisance who should be barred from watching their plays in rehearsal, on the grounds that they are out of place amidst the sacred rites of production and that their presence puts off the actors, still persists among a certain type of over-bearing, thoughtless and usually unconfident director. To deprive the creator of the play of the pleasure and thrill of seeing it gradually coming to life is ungracious and rather childishly stupid. The value of the author's full co-operation has already been emphasised. It is in the early rehearsals that this can be most profitably exercised. He can see for himself where a line may need adjusting to ease the flow of the dialogue, or cutting because in performance a look or a gesture has made it superfluous. He is immediately available to clear up any points that may need elucidation, and to discuss and, if agreed, carry out any further textual changes the director may request.

It is at this stage of the proceedings that any 'favourite lines' which have got past the pre-rehearsal conferences will, with any luck, be eliminated. By 'favourite lines' are meant those splendidly chiselled literary gems which may well have given the author most delight in writing but which, un-happily, are extraneous to the context, impede the flow of the dialogue, and are a drag on the development of the play. An experienced director will spot them very early on and will begin using all his tact and cunning to persuade the author to cut them. It is unlikely that he will have succeeded over all of them until they are shown up in rehearsal. The reluctance of the author to cut them often becomes evident when, after the London or New York run, the play is pub-lished in book form with many of the 'favourite lines' put back. This is a foolish practice, principally because it ham-pers directors of subsequent productions who work from the published book. They are loath to cut lines, however jarring they may seem, which were apparently used in what may have been a London or New York smash hit. They are not in a position to discuss the matter with the author and their productions suffer.

It is very important that any notes or suggestions that the author may want to make to the cast should be channelled through the director. It is for him to decide whether they accord with what he wants and, if so, to judge the appro-priate time to pass them on to the individuals concerned. The rule and the reasons for it should be made clear to the author before the rehearsals begin and should be strictly adhered to. It can, however, present difficulties. Although actors know well enough that they must receive their instructions and guidance on how to play their parts from the director only, they sometimes anxiously seek reassurance by getting the author into a corner and plying him with questions. He, having no wish to seem unhelpful, answers them as best he can. What he says may well be related to the character as originally conceived by him, and at variance with the character which the director is seeking to build up from within the actor playing it. This can only lead to confusion in the actor's mind, and sorting it out will waste precious time.

The inexperienced author should be warned not to expect instantaneous results. One such, a down-to-earth north-country lady who had written a most amusing first comedy (and went on eventually to write a West End smash hit), reproached the leading man after the first rehearsal with: 'I thought I'd written a funny part, but you aren't making it sound funny at all.'

It is sound policy for the author to be absent during the middle period of rehearsal when the actors have just put down their books and are struggling with their lines. If the author is there, they become over-conscious of being off-text, lose confidence, get worse and waste time being apologetic. Moreover, at that stage, when the play seems awful, their own parts unplayable, and the entire proceedings a woeful waste of time, they like to feel free to express themselves forcibly without fear of giving offence. When that phase is over and the production is beginning to take real shape, the author's presence is again desirable for making any final textual adjustments either requested by the director or suggested by himself. During the final run-through of rehearsals, the director may well ask him what further steps he thinks can still be taken to bring their joint effort to full fruition.

There is, of course, the possibility that by this time they will not be speaking to each other, the director claiming that he has been totally frustrated by the author's myopic, obstinate refusal to make the drastic changes he has demanded, the author cursing the director and the actors for completely wrecking his play. Either may be true. When such an unhappy disruption of a relationship does occur there are usually faults on both sides. But it *does* sometimes happen that an author refuses to accept the unwritten law that in all matters (except actual text) pertaining to the production the director must have the last word and that even the text is negotiable, with only the *very* last word being the author's.

It also sometimes happens that plays are destroyed by inept direction, shoddy presentation or inadequate acting. This is an occupational hazard which the author must accept when he seeks to have his play produced. It is likely to be of little solace to him that the director's reputation will probably go down in the wreck. It must be added that the 'wreck' is often only in the mind of the author, unable to accept that his brainchild has grown into anything so totally different from what he had conceived. If others do not share his view, it may well be that a thriving box office will console him.

In the mid-thirties a play called *Young England* had a long London run. Its author was an elderly moralist whose earnest intention was to extol virtue and condemn vice. The play was so bad and its message so badly overstated that it became a target for certain wits who built up a stock of ribald interruptions which came to be accepted by the actors as part of the text. In a very short time *Young England* became a cult to which all London flocked. As people jostled for tickets, the author stood in the foyer exhorting them in a loud voice to take his play seriously. This was regarded as part of the fun. His plight would have deserved sympathy had it not been that, in addition to being the play's author, he was its backer and manager. Thus the decision rested with him alone whether to put an end to the nightly desecration of his masterpiece or to continue to make a fortune from it.

Though it is seldom that the director of a revival will meet the author, much of the foregoing may be worth his consideration. If it does no more, it will remind him that, present or not present, alive or dead, the author is the creator of the play and as such should be treated with respect.

CHAPTER FOUR

Relationship with the Designer and Other Relevant Matters

Every play requires a setting, sometimes simple, sometimes elaborate. It may be primarily decorative; on the other hand, it may make a direct and positive contribution to the action of the play. Whatever its nature, it must accord in style and in functional suitability with the director's conception of the production as a whole.

The person responsible for it is the designer. As it is essential that they should work in the closest harmony, he should, if possible, be nominated by the director. Their relationship may vary from the director knowing what he wants in every detail and giving precise instructions which the designer carries out, to the designer being given a more or less free hand in all except purely functional matters. The first can only work satisfactorily if the director is himself a trained and experienced designer, the second only if the director has implicit faith in the designer's ability to produce what will be totally acceptable to him. (Possibly, of course, he himself is devoid of ideas and does not contribute even constructive criticism, because he has none to make. Every director, however brilliant, must be allowed at least one deficiency and this, poor soul, could be his. It must be admitted that it is a fairly serious one.) The usual situation lies somewhere between these two extremes, with director and designer sparking ideas off one another and the latter carrying out the final answer approved by the former.

Most often they get together for a discussion as soon as the director has studied the play in sufficient detail to have a clear idea of how he is going to produce it, and the designer has had an opportunity to consider it from his point of view. The director will say what general style, shape and structure he wants, and what 'practicalities' (entrances, windows, different levels, etc) will be needed and where. They pool their ideas as to how these requirements are to be achieved, with the designer probably scribbling little sketch plans as they talk.

If the play demands a straightforward conventional single set, there are unlikely to be any problems from the director's point of view. After the general style—and possibly the colour—has been agreed, the designer will be left to work out some way of bringing individuality to it without making it freakish or otherwise obtrusive. It cannot be emphasised enough, that the setting must always, save in the most exceptional circumstances, provide the background to the play and not in any way dominate the production. The dedicated stage designer derives his satisfaction as an artist from his creation's fitness for its purpose, and not from its virtuosity. Should he allow himself to be carried away and ignore this all-important precept, it will be up to the director to curb his over-exuberance as soon as it becomes apparent.

If the set contributes positively to the action of the play, the director clearly becomes more involved in the detail of its design. If the play has many scenes, the method of presentation may well be fundamental to the way the action moves and must, therefore, be predominantly a matter for the director's decision. Within the method chosen the designer will usually be given as free a hand as possible to exercise his talent and ingenuity. The methods are many and the choice will be governed by such considerations as (*a*) the nature of the play; (*b*) the possible need for continuity of action; (*c*) the need, or lack of need, for such things as realistic furniture and similar heavy properties; (*d*) the dimensions and facilities of the stage on which the play is to be produced; (*e*) the lines of sight from the auditorium (Fig 1 and 2); (*f*) the minimum number of stage hands available; (*g*) the sophistication, or lack of it, of the potential audience; finally, and not least important, (*h*) the financial and other resources of the organisation presenting the play.

'Conventional' scenery (consisting of painted canvas flats cleated together for interiors, and hinged wings, back cloths and ground rows for exteriors), or modifications of it, may well be found most suitable for plays without continuity of action requiring no more than, say, three different sets and with appropriate breaks in the action allowing adequate time to change them. The time may be substantially shortened by the use of such aids as a revolving stage, wheeled trucks and a counterweight flying system, or by setting one scene inside the other.

The value of a revolving stage or wheeled truck in changing conventional sets is that they allow scope for more elaborately built sets than would be possible if they had to be dismantled and assembled at each change. Moreover, they move not only the sets but the furniture. A revolving stage

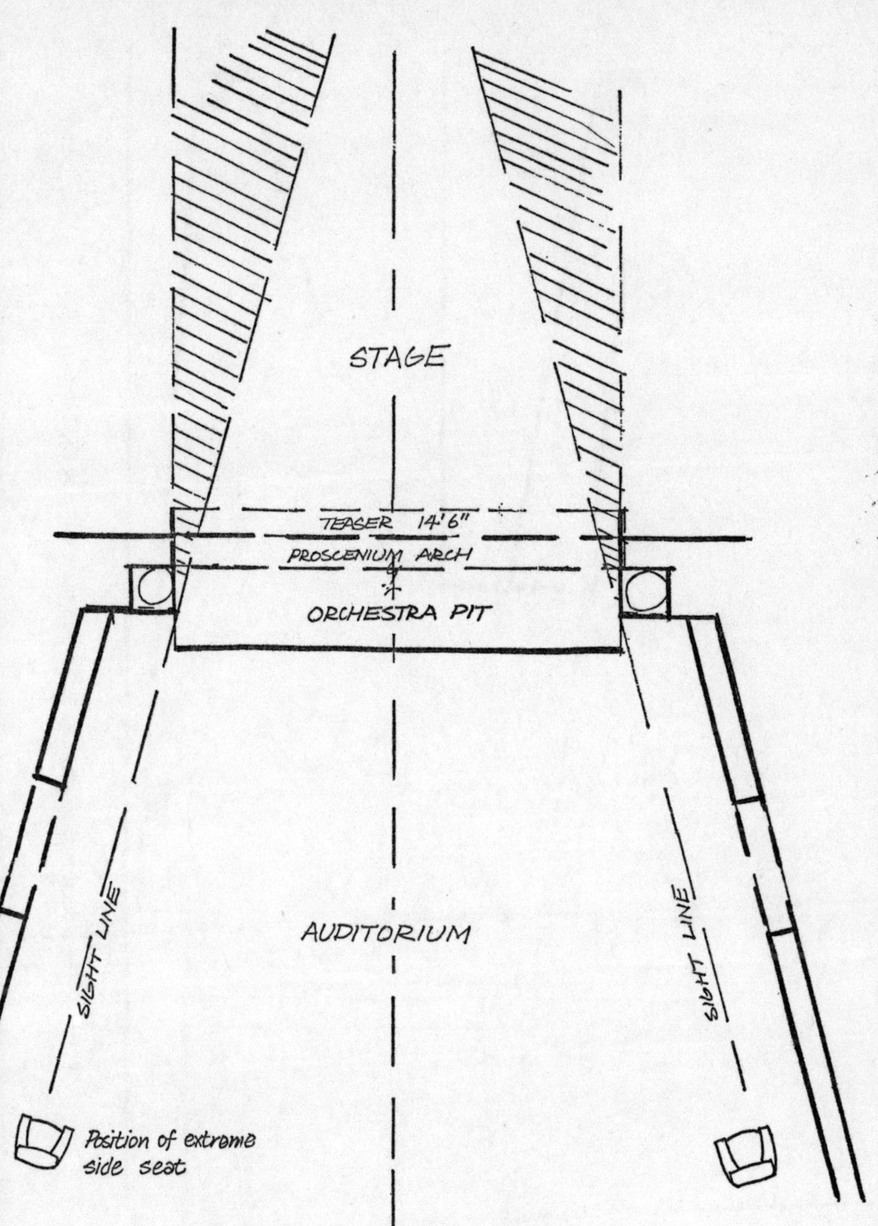

Fig 1. Plan showing sight lines

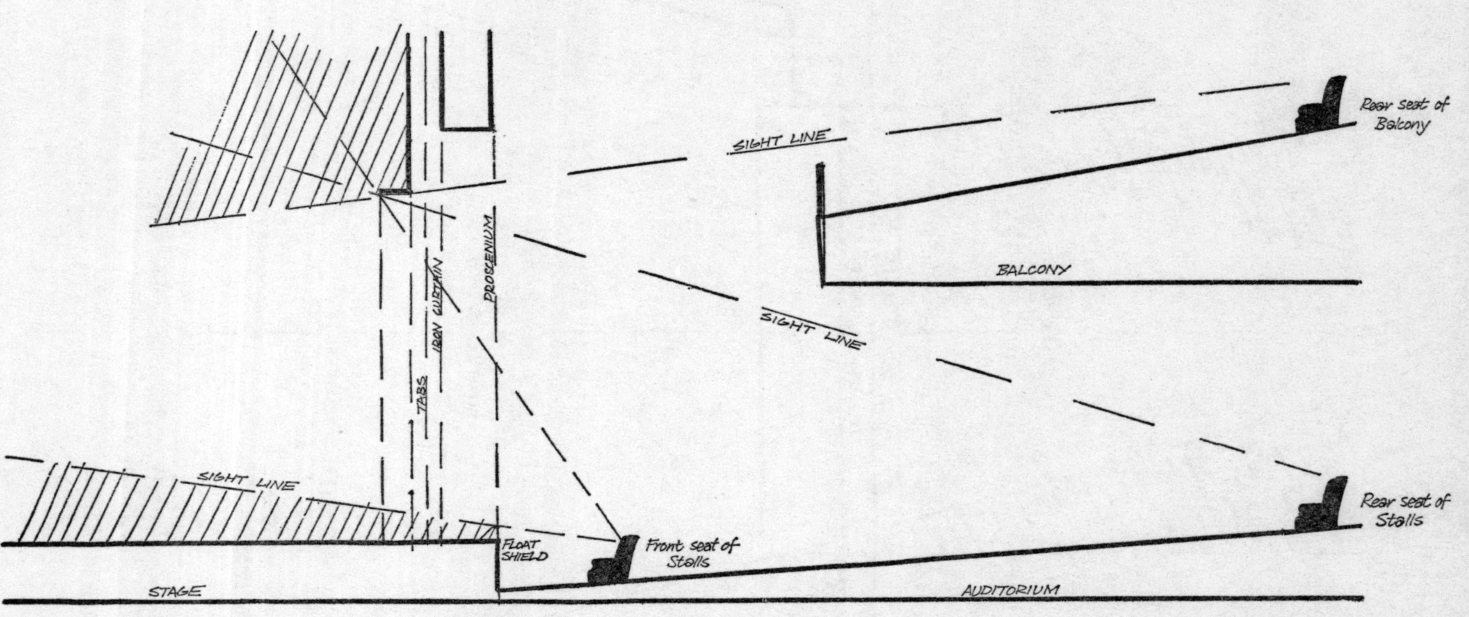

Fig 2. Section through stage and auditorium showing sight lines

(or 'revolve') is, however, not quite such a panacea for all quick-change problems as may be imagined by those who covet but have not yet used one. It has its limitations and drawbacks. These arise from the fundamental fact that a revolve is a circle and the stage in which it turns can be regarded as a rectangle formed by the line between each corner of the proscenium, tangential to the circumference of the revolve, and two imaginary lines running upstage from each corner marking the boundary of the acting area (Fig 3). The set is an irregular segment of the circle with its outer edges on the circumference. Between them and the boundary of the acting area there will be a gap (shaded on diagram) which will vary in distance according to the relative width of the proscenium opening and the diameter of the revolve. If the diameter is less than the proscenium opening, the gap can never close (Fig 3a). If the two are the same, the gap will close along the line of the diameter, that is half-way up the revolve (Fig 3b). As the relative length of the diameter increases, so the point of 'no gap' will come further downstage (Fig 3c). Only if the diameter is at least twice the width of the proscenium opening, requiring a far bigger stage than is to be found in most theatres, will there be no perceptible gap (Fig 3d). In other words, the front of the set would be able to fill the whole width of the proscenium opening as it normally would if no revolve were used.

In practice, the diameter of most revolves is very little wider than the proscenium arch. Thus, the problem is to fill the gap. If it is essential that the changes are made in the shortest possible time, the extension of the 'tormentors' or masking pieces from the proscenium corner to the edge of the revolve is the most straightforward solution. They can be cleated to the outside edges of each set as it comes round. It must then be accepted that the openings of the sets will be

D

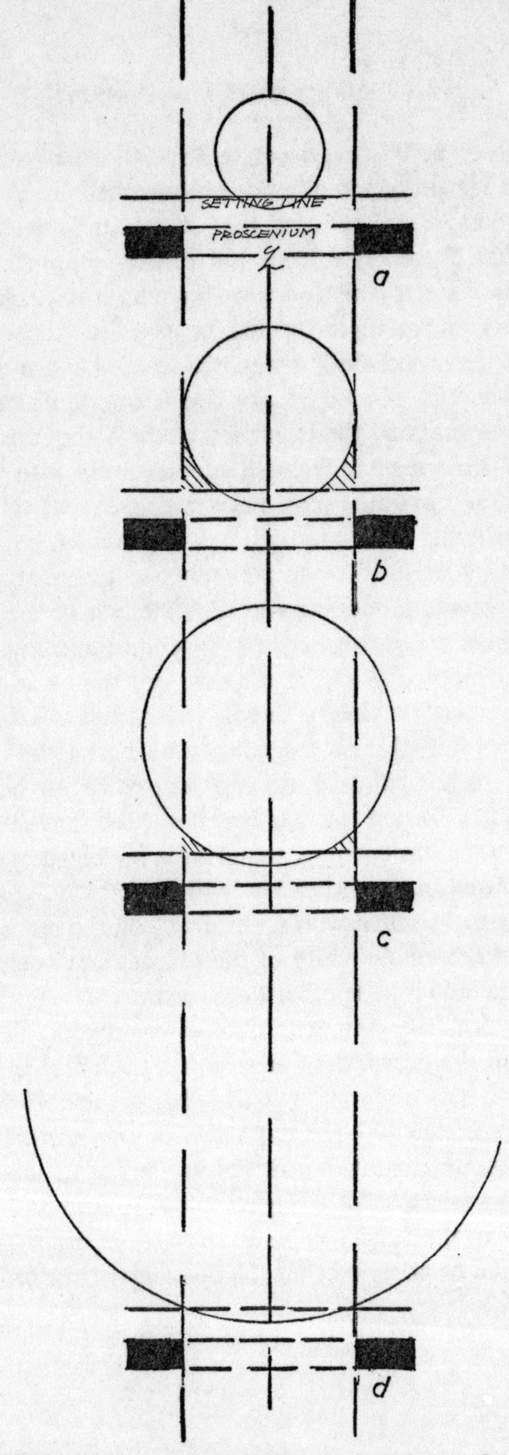

Fig 3. Diagram showing relation between proscenium and 'revolves' of differing diameters

several feet narrower, with possible consequences to overall dimensions and lines of sight. If full width is more important than the speed of the changes, flats forming the extreme edges of each set, and furniture if needed, can be positioned between the revolve and the masking piece.

For certain productions, a revolve used in conjunction with a cyclorama and three-dimensional scenery can be extremely effective. It allows for continuous action; and, merely by moving the revolve a fraction of a full turn at a time to show various facets of the built pieces, a great number of different settings can be obtained at a minimum of cost and effort. (A notable example was Olivier's famous production of *Antony and Cleopatra* at the old St James's Theatre, London, in the early 1950s.) The old pantomime technique, or an elaboration of it, of 'full set followed by a front cloth while the next full set is being mounted' still has something to commend it for plays which are suitably constructed; for example, much of Shakespeare and many musicals. The projection of slides, either from the back or front, on to a cyclorama or screens has been in use for many years, especially in the large theatres and opera houses of Europe. The method presents difficulties—in particular, of lighting the acting area adequately without diminishing the effectiveness of the projected image. New techniques and stronger lamps may lead to its much wider use in the future.

Television has had a profound effect on the techniques of play-writing for the theatre. Many dramatists no longer feel themselves bound by the old discipline imposed by having to sustain long scenes in no more than two or three settings. They take the much freer and easier course of writing a great number of short scenes, more or less ignoring considerations of time and place. The flexibility of television not only

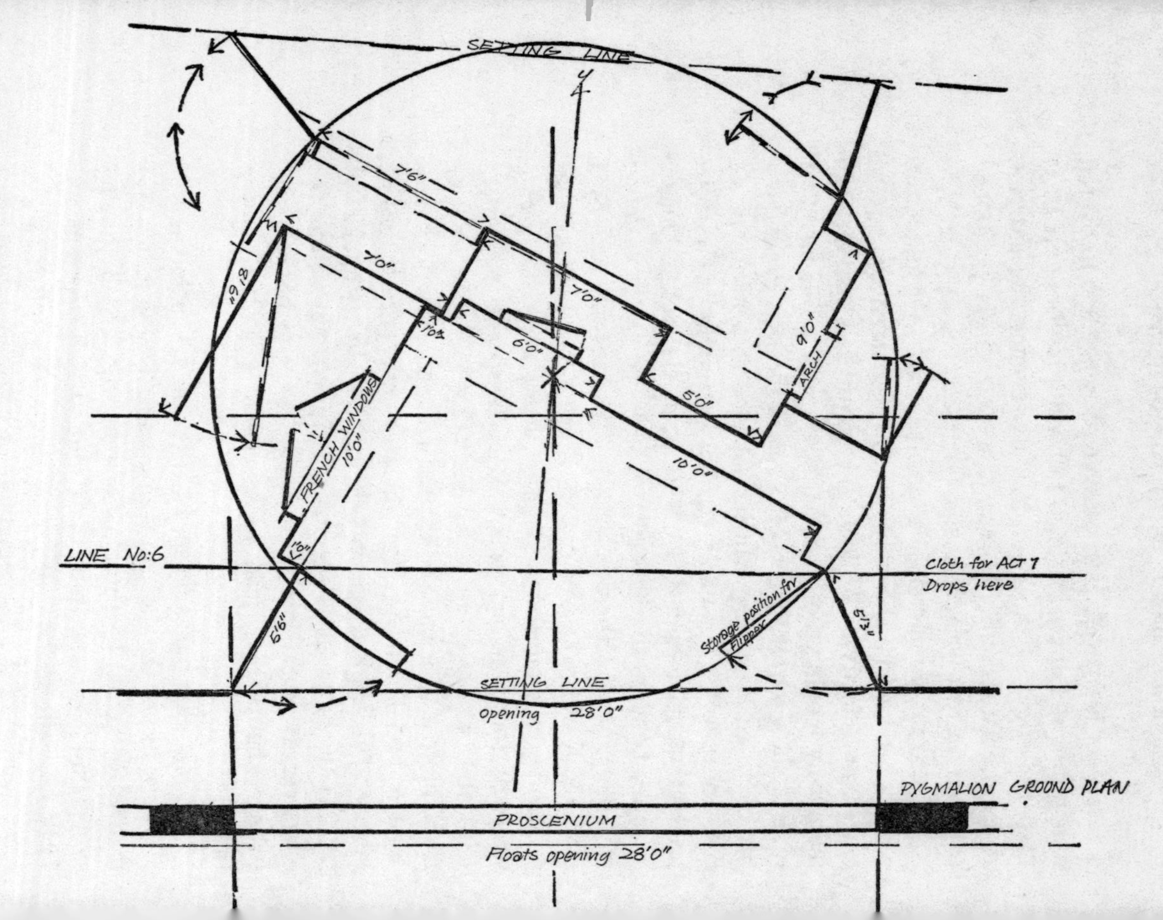
SETTING LINE
7'6"
7'0"
7'0"
6'0"
9'0"
ARCH
5'0"
10'0"
6'9"
FRENCH WINDOWS
10'0"
LINE No:6
1'0"
Cloth for Act 1
Drops here
6'6"
Storage position for
Fireplace
5'3"
SETTING LINE
opening 28'0"
PYGMALION GROUND PLAN
PROSCENIUM
Floats opening 28'0"

permits this but makes a virtue of it. In the theatre, it is a much more difficult matter and no wholly satisfactory method has been found to stage plays of this kind.

The one usually favoured by the dramatist in his stage directions is the 'composite set'. It may be added that he has seldom bothered to work out the practicalities of his suggestions in terms of the dimensions of most theatres' stages. The problem is that, however 'composite', there is only a limited space available on any stage, even when using multiple levels. If, as so often happens, the dramatist ignores that fact, by the time one has obeyed his instructions and put into that space, say, living room, bedroom, bathroom and kitchen of old so-and-so's house, somebody else's garage, a hill top outside the city and the inside of a church in Antwerp, there is precious little room in any single acting area to swing a cat (Figs 5 and 6). The designer may also be hard put to juxtapose totally unrelated locales in such a way as to enable the director to keep the movement of the play reasonably fluid, coherent and smooth. One can imagine during an early plotting rehearsal, with the multiple levels indicated only by different coloured tapes covering the same area of flat floor, a plaintive cry from one of the actors: 'How do I get from the living-room to the loo?' and the answer from the harassed director, quickly consulting his ground plan: 'Through area 2, that is, let me see now, the garage, and on to area 6—that is the hill without a city wall —and straight on through area 4—that is Antwerp Church.' Then soothingly, but without much conviction: 'You'll see it will work out quite naturally in the actual set.'

It would, of course, be wrong to suggest that most or even many authors make such impossible demands on the designer —but even at their best, composite sets tend to be cramping both to the director in working out his production and to the

Fig 5. Design of the composite set asked for by the dramatist

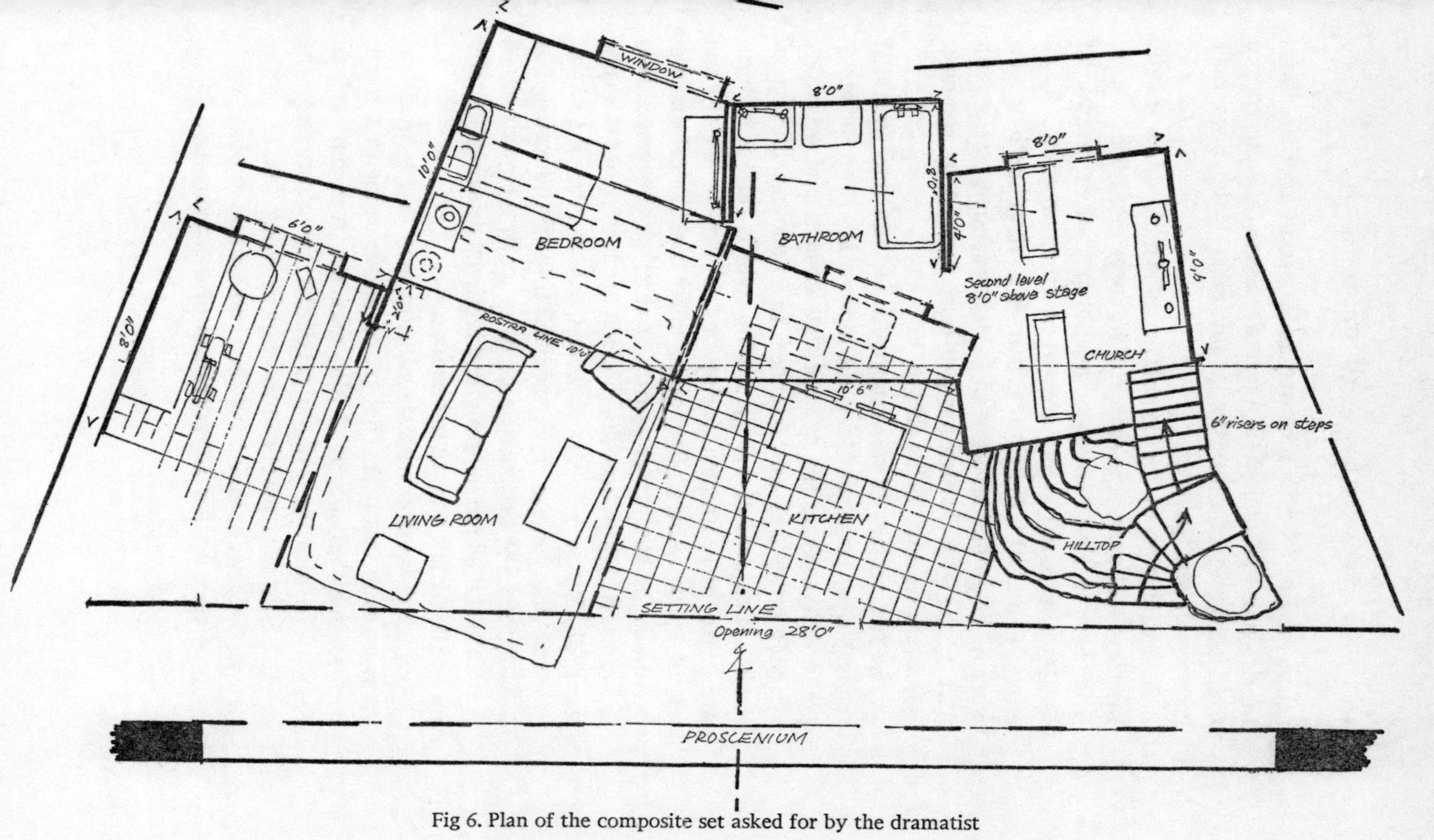

Fig 6. Plan of the composite set asked for by the dramatist

actors moving from one constricted space to another. From the designer's point of view, ingenuity has to take precedence over aesthetic considerations, and clear sight lines over creation of atmosphere.

A modification of the composite set which, when it suits the play, will overcome many of the snags mentioned above, is for each locale to be represented by part of the overall set but for the actual acting area to be common to all. As an example, an actor indicates that he is in the church at Antwerp by beginning his scene in it. He then moves to the main part of the stage, which has just been vacated by the chap ostensibly working in his garage.

Another variant of the composite set and one which, if the resources are available, is the most satisfactory for many plays, derives from the precept that scenery and props are symbols only, and not intended to create an illusion of reality. It consists of a single set into which various features are added or subtracted as required, either by 'flying', the use of trucks, hinged flats and similar mechanical devices, or simply by the actors as part of their performance. Two famous and highly successful London productions of this type were *Oh, What A Lovely War* and *A Man For All Seasons*.

When the general style and structure of the setting has been agreed, the designer proceeds to work them out in the form of detailed ground plans and sectional drawings, usually on a scale of half an inch to one foot.

Further discussion with the director may lead to modifications or even complete changes of mind: what in a rough scribble may seem a good idea may not turn out well in detail. The director will, in particular, be scrutinising the exact position of practicalities which, when related to the rest of the design, may have been moved out of place. Or it may be that further consideration of his production intentions has caused him to change his mind as to where they should be.

Next, the designer makes a model of the set or sets, again usually to a scale of half an inch to the foot, which will greatly assist the director both in his preparatory plotting and in showing the actors during early rehearsals exactly what he means. It also enables the actors to keep a picture in their mind's eye of the surroundings in which they will eventually be performing. Finally, the model will almost certainly go to the scenery workshops, where it will guide the builders and painters of the actual set as to what the detailed drawings and designs from which they are working will eventually add up to. Indeed, to save time and effort, the working drawings are often dispensed with and the model used instead. This is unwise, however, unless the designer is continuously on the spot to explain or elaborate what he had intended.

In addition to the actual sets, the designer is responsible for the whole decor which goes into them—furniture, curtains, floor coverings, ornaments. These should also be discussed with the director and his approval obtained—especially of practical props like chairs, sofas, beds and tables which will be used in the action of the play. Whether these are to be hired, borrowed or bought, it usually saves time in the long run if the director and designer choose them together.

The wearing apparel of the actors on stage principally concerns the director as regards its suitability for the characters they are depicting and the settings in which they will be working. In modern plays, unless he considers himself an expert on the subject he would usually be sensible to discuss the matter in general terms with the individuals concerned, and leave the actual choice to them, perhaps in consultation

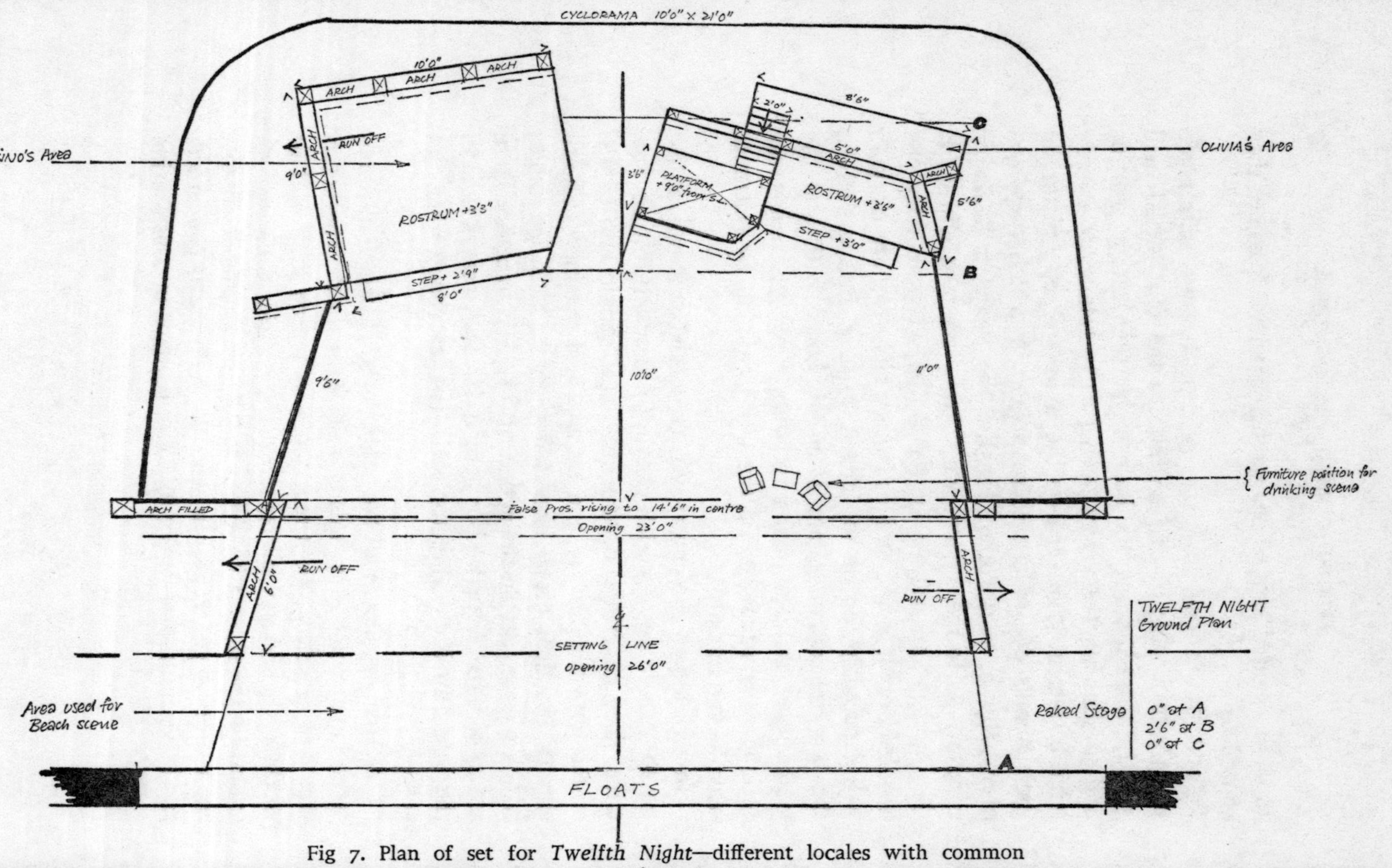

Fig 7. Plan of set for *Twelfth Night*—different locales with common setting area

with the head of the wardrobe department (if there is one) or someone else with 'dress sense'. In a slap-up production with the ladies' clothes being provided at cut rates by a famous *haute couturier* intent upon getting maximum publicity in return for his discount, the problem may well be to prevent the production becoming a dress show.

If the play is in 'costume', it is again usually wise for the director, having decided upon the precise period and general style, to leave the job to the experts: the designer and dressmaker, if the costumes are to be specially made for the production, or the theatrical costumier if they are to be hired. One point he must insist upon if the costumes are new is that they should be comfortable for the actors to work in. This is particularly important when there is a great deal of movement involved. Too often designers in their zeal or in their determination to be totally accurate in the matter of 'period', forget that stage costumes should conform to the requirements of stage technique—that is, they should allow their wearer to move and breathe freely and not be overburdened with excessive weight.

It need hardly be said that however free a hand the director gives to others in providing the clothes for his production, he must reserve to himself the right of final approval and have no qualms about withholding it.

CHAPTER FIVE

Casting the Play

The method of casting a play will very much depend upon the nature of the organisation presenting it. If it is a repertory company with a resident group of actors, the director's room for manœuvre is clearly very limited; in fact, his job will be to allot the parts as suitably as possible. With amateur groups the method will be the same, although the chances are that the field of choice will be somewhat wider. When casting a professional company for a single production, one's choice is only limited by the availability of actors, the sum allowed for salaries in the production's budget and, possibly, the nature of the engagement. The effectiveness of the casting within that choice very much depends upon the perspicacity and professional judgement of the director. (For purposes of discussion, it is assumed that his judgement will not be overridden by the management's insistance on star names or by the author's right to veto.)

Even within the limitations of a resident company or amateur group, there is usually some choice between one actor or another for playing a particular part, and in making it the director should ask himself the same two basic questions he would if he had the whole acting profession at his disposal: which actor will be most acceptable and convincing to the audience as the character he will be representing? And which is most capable of bringing out the full potential of the part?

In looking for the answers, the director must get his priorities right. For every part, certain qualities of talent and characteristics of personality are essential and others are desirable. Outside these two categories there may be preferences, but these are immaterial to the issue. Which qualities and characteristics come under each category will vary according to the type of part. For instance, in some parts the semblance of a particular age is essential, in others it is desirable and in others immaterial. To take two widely different parts as examples of how such an analysis works:

1. Lord Fancourt Babberley (Babs) in *Charley's Aunt*
   Essentials: Talent for farce, semblance of youth, attractive personality
   Desirables: Not tall, educated voice, extrovert
   Immaterial: Looks, colouring or ability to play anything but farce

2. *Hamlet*
   Essentials: Talent for portraying deep emotion, semblance of youth, intelligence, strong and flexible voice, physical stamina
   Desirables: Pleasing voice, suggestion of breeding, introvert
   Immaterial: Physique, colouring, ability to play other types of part

Such an approach to casting comes somewhere between the assumption that a good actor can play any kind of part and what is, usually scornfully, termed 'type-casting'. It recognises that, however talented an actor may be, he is almost certainly able to play some kind of parts better than others and that, in a highly competitive world, these are the parts for which he is most likely to be cast and in which, through experience, he has become most expert. If his special skill is in farce, then he fulfils the first essential requirement of Babs; if in emotional parts, that of Hamlet.

This is not to deny the possibility that the same actor *could* play either. John Gielgud is generally recognised as having been not only the greatest Hamlet of his generation, but the most notable John Worthing in *The Importance of Being Earnest*. But pressures of one kind or another tend to force most professional actors into a degree of specialisation which they may well not desire and which very frequently blunts, through lack of practice, their skill in playing other kinds of parts. A director may well spot that a particular actor has grown stale in playing the same kind of part too often and decide against engaging him to play it yet again. On the other hand he may be perspicacious and bold enough to cast right against an actor's usual line of part in the hope of producing an electrifying performance. He has bargained on putting the actor on his mettle and forcing him to delve deeper into himself than he probably has for years, rekindling his basic instinct to act. Like all risks, of course, it may not come off and thus could even ruin the entire production. Generally speaking, mindful of his responsibilities to those who are employing him, to the rest of the company, to the author, and not least to the public, the director plays safe and satisfies himself as far as he possibly can that the essential talents and characteristics are there.

To cast on physical appearance and 'off-stage' personality *can* work out to the satisfaction of an audience—but with certain provisos: first, that the actor has sufficient talent to

'play himself', generally acknowledged to be the most difficult form of acting; second, that the play is sufficiently good
in itself not to require the contribution of a creative performance; third, that the audience has not seen him too often
'as himself' to accept him as the character in the play. From
the director's point of view, type-casting of this kind gives
his creative imagination little scope. He knows from the start
exactly what performance he is going to get and can sit back
and watch it happen with a minimum of effort—or fun.

Nowhere more conclusively than in the theatre does one
find proof that beauty (whether male or female) is only skin-
deep. Much disastrous casting results from this being overlooked. It is what is behind an actor's looks that really
matters, and if, as so often happens, there is no quality of
personality to match the physical appearance and no acting
talent to project this quality, even Venus and Apollo together would leave an audience cold. The converse is also
very true: an actor may by sheer conviction transcend the
physical. There is a well-known story that when Edith Evans,
who has been endowed with every grace except good looks,
was cast when in her mid-forties to play Rosalind in *As You
Like It*, she used to stare at herself in the mirror for a long
time before each performance, repeating to herself: 'I am
young and beautiful, I am young and beautiful.' Having
convinced herself, she convinced the audience.

Moreover, in the theatre, in contrast to the cinema and TV
where the searching lens of a camera in close-up makes
deception more difficult, what may be called 'mechanical
aids'—make-up, wigs, 'falsies', etc—can go far towards providing the physical requirements of a character. In a very
successful musical in London in the middle 50s, the leading
part was a synthesis of every glamorous Hollywood dumb
blonde of the period. Besides looks, it required someone of

outstanding acting talent, with a sharp intellect able to give full value to satire, and an ability to sing with meticulous articulation. Type-casting in the normally accepted sense would have been a contradiction in terms. Yet the actress who eventually played it and scored a sensational success had originally been turned down because off-stage she lacked glamour. It had been overlooked how synthetic this particular attribute can be.

Having said all that, physical characteristics must inevitably come into it. Not all actresses have the ability of Edith Evans, and not every part requiring a beautiful girl has the quality of Rosalind through which she may shine. By and large, it would be perverse deliberately to choose a plain girl to play Helen of Troy, a short man to play Goliath, a thin boy to play Billy Bunter. There are, too, certain theatrical conventions which it is wise to follow unless there is a very good reason to flout them. For example, although in life a husband shorter than his wife is accepted without comment, in the theatre it is regarded as comic. Therefore, in casting two characters who are romantically linked, it is normal to engage an actor who is taller than the actress.

The importance of age also depends to some extent on convention. It is axiomatic that no girl of fifteen could satisfactorily play Juliet, and an audience is therefore prepared to accept an actress twice that age or more. French actresses over sixty are accepted by their audiences as young girls, as indeed they used to be in England when Julia Neilson and Lady Martin Harvey toured the provinces. Many repertory audiences have accustomed themselves, *faute de mieux*, to accept the playing of middle-aged and elderly characters by actors whom they know to be in their early twenties. What is important, especially nowadays when films and television have set new standards of realism, is that an actor should have at least a credible semblance to the age of the character he is portraying. As in the case of beauty, mechanical aids can be used, but this should be with discretion. Young actors with heavy lines of make-up across their foreheads and heavy shadings in the hollows of their cheeks look just a grotesque mess; the onetime much-used device of streaking the hair with white grease paint also lacked conviction. But splendid wigs with lace fronts, and other hairpieces, moustaches, beards, side whiskers and eyebrows now obtainable can go far to adding age to a young face. What still need careful watching, because they tend more than anything else to give away true age, are the neck and hands.

Assuming he knows his business, the author will have given the characters in the play varying degrees of importance and strength of personality which will result in the right relationship and dramatic balance between them. The director, when casting, should seek to preserve this balance. To 'over-cast' a minor character may throw the whole production out of tune. 'All-star casts', though meat and drink for the publicity department and often for the box office, tend to be unsatisfactory in most other respects.

Although the director of a repertory company or an amateur group is necessarily limited in his choice of actors when casting an individual play, he will probably be directly concerned in recruiting new members for the company or group. In doing so, he may well adopt the same methods as the director who is casting a professional production from scratch. The sources of potential talent available to him are likely to be:

1. Actors with whom he has worked in the past. Assuming that they got on well together, and all else being equal, he is likely to give preference to them over actors whose per-

E

sonal characteristics and method of working he does not know.

2. Actors he has seen in plays produced by others. These may range from great stars to some small-part players whose performance impressed him.

3. Actors who have been recommended to him by others whose judgement he trusts: producers, directors, actors—or agents. The last named 'represent' actors, looking after their business and doing their best to obtain them work in return for a percentage—usually ten per cent, but sometimes more—of their earnings. Their recommendations should be regarded with caution as naturally they are likely to be heavily biased.

4. Actors listed in such professional publications as *The Spotlight Casting Directory*, which contains the photographs and sometimes the credits of many professional actors. Most directors regard it as an invaluable reminding service—to go through *Spotlight* is usually the first action of any professional casting session. But few would be rash enough even to consider an unknown on the strength of his photograph alone. One learns from experience how time-wasting that usually is.

5. Actors—or, in the case of amateurs, would-be actors—whom he has interviewed or auditioned. The value of auditions for actors is, incidentally, highly questionable. It is different for singers or dancers, both of whom are required to show a precise talent which can generally be judged fairly accurately, provided a reasonable allowance is made for nerves. But a talent for acting is anything but precise, as will be shown in a later chapter. And at the heart of it, without which nothing else really matters, is the one thing an audition cannot show—the ability to 'get across' to an audience. The better the actor and the more important the

part is to him, the more likely he is to be gripped at an audition with a kind of nervous paralysis, a feeling of total unreality. His throat dry, his brain numb, he is conscious only of the cold, disembodied voice coming out of the darkness of the auditorium giving him directions as to what he is to read or recite, or whatever form of torture he is being put to. The less good the actor, that is the less sensitive, the less he is likely to be affected and, on the face of it, the better audition he will give. Much bad acting to be seen around can be attributed to this simple fact. Those things which an audition may show—physique, personality, quality of voice, intelligence and, in particular, suitability for the part for which the actor is being considered—can be more readily assessed at an interview, during which the wise director will deliberately create as relaxed an atmosphere as possible.

The most practical way to proceed is to make a list against each character of all names which suggest themselves or are suggested from these various sources. Consider them all carefully and then number them in priority of choice. Start with the leading parts and as each character is cast, move on to the next most important, possibly adjusting priorities to keep the cast in balance. It is wise to allow as much time as possible (professional actors tend to sniff round a new part with the suspicion of a cat deciding on the site of its accouchement), to exercise great patience and not to be panicked into wrong decisions by a long run of failures to get the actors one originally wanted. It is not too much to say that the secret of any successful production depends first and foremost upon its casting.

CHAPTER SIX

Relationship with Actors

Without doubt the most important, the most fascinating, sometimes the most difficult and usually the most rewarding part of a director's job is the handling of actors. They are the predominant medium through which he brings his production to life. It is, therefore, all-important that he should seek to establish with each member of the cast a close mutual understanding and trust. With certain individuals this may not prove easy—for any one of a hundred reasons, the two sides may not hit it off. It is up to the director to take positive measures to clear up such a situation.

Actors are, for the most part, sensitive, vulnerable and unsure of themselves (those who appear to be otherwise are usually putting up a bluff in self-defence). The reason is that acting is an intangible and elusive form of artistic expression—a complicated process of the actor working out with his conscious mind what he imagines to be the thoughts, feelings and idiosyncrasies of the character he has been given to portray, subsequently absorbing them into his subconscious so that in performance the expression of them with his voice, physique and personality will appear to be coming from within himself. At the same time, his conscious mind will, as it were, be sitting outside the performance and controlling it technically. What makes the actor unsure of himself is the fear that at some point this complicated process may break down; that he may become as Shakespeare put it,

> As an unperfect actor on the stage
> who with his fear is put beside his part.

It is one of the director's primary jobs to try to remove this uncertainty and give the actors confidence in themselves. This may well be most effectively achieved by persuading them to have confidence in him. He should begin by showing at the first rehearsal that he has done his homework properly —that he knows exactly what he wants and how he is going to get it. He is expected to know all the answers. Those he *does* know he should give with complete confidence. Those he doesn't, he should parry—a certain degree of bluff is necessary and pardonable. He should on no account *flounder*. Actors seeking reassurance rightly mistrust a director who is vague, evasive, contradictory and woolly-minded.

He must come with an apparently clear idea as to how he thinks each part should be played by the particular actor concerned. This will provide a basis from which to answer any questions the actor asks. The latter will almost certainly have already brought his own imagination, experience, feelings and intelligence to bear on the matter. The result may well be entirely different from what the director has envisaged (and even more from what the author first conceived). The director may decide that much of the proposed interpretation is valid and in the course of rehearsals will build upon it. On the other hand, there are likely to be some aspects of it that are out of harmony with the production as he intends it to be. These he will seek to alter, choosing the right time and occasion to do so.

The analogy is frequently made between the director and the conductor of an orchestra, but it is in many ways misleading. The conductor is dealing with players of instruments producing notes of a strictly defined nature. The feeling, technique and timing which the individual player can bring to his playing is or should be in response to the conductor's requirements, but the instrument from which the actual notes are produced does not vary. The director of a play is not dealing with anything as precise. The actor has nothing so concrete as a fiddle to latch on to. The only instrument he has is himself: face, eyes, mouth, voice, bodily movement and posture—invoked, as has been said, by a subtle interplay between the conscious and subconscious mind to give expression to an idea, a thought, a feeling. To get what he wants from so complex and imprecise an instrument, the director must use methods much less direct and probably more subtle than the conductor needs to employ.

The second important difference between conductor and director is that the former is very much in command during the actual performance, whereas the latter is a mere bystander once the curtain goes up. The actor is out on his own and the influence of the director on what he does and how he does it is not imparted by the commanding downsweep of a baton but by more or less automatic recollection of what has been said, discussed and practised during the rehearsal period. Moreover, the crux of the art of acting—the establishment of a reciprocal emotional relationship between actor and audience, which by its nature will influence and modify his performance—must necessarily be outside the director's control. Looking from a purely functional point of view, the conductor, provided he obtains the right note played the way he wants it, does not necessarily care who plays it. It is the musician's talent only with which he is concerned, not to any appreciable extent his personality. On the other hand, in the process of acting, talent and personality are inextricably mixed, and in obtaining what he wants the director will be very much involved with the idiosyncrasies of each individual.

Actors tend to fall into categories, each of which needs different handling. At one extreme is the purely instinctive actor, very often with no great intelligence, who may not consciously understand more than the bare outline of the character he is playing, yet brings to it a kind of sixth sense which infuses it with life and meaning. It would be useless attempting to push him along intellectual lines. He'll probably not grasp what one is talking about and become over-anxious and develop a sense of inferiority. He should be talked to in terms he *can* understand, given general guidelines along which he will find his own interpretation of the part. This may well be a joy to watch, with never a movement, a gesture, a look, out of place: pure acting uncomplicated by cerebral promptings, but obviously with a limited range.

One such actor was for several years a most valuable member of the Windsor Theatre Company. He gave many outstanding performances in a wide range of parts. He had, however, a terror of 'classic' plays. Told that he was to play Bottom in *A Midsummer Nights Dream*, for which he was ideally suited, he became so agitated that he fainted. The management reluctantly used someone else in the part but gently warned him that in future he would be required to carry out the terms of his contract to 'play as cast' or leave the company.

Some months later, he was cast for Sir Wilfull Witwoud in Congreve's *The Way of the World*. He tackled the part with the resolution and apprehension of a soldier going into battle. As far as was possible in the limited rehearsal time available for a very complicated production, the mysteries of the text were patiently unravelled for him. For instance, when he came to the speech to Mirabell: ' 'Sheart, an you talk of an instrument, sir, I have an old fox at my thigh shall hack your instrument of ram vellam to shreds, sir. Therefore withdraw your instrument, sir, or by'r Lady I shall draw mine', he was told to slap his hand on the hilt of his sword. There was a pause:

'Will I be wearing a sword?'

"What do you imagine the old fox at your thigh refers to?'

Pause.

'I thought it was a little dog.'

His eventual performance was so convincing, so richly comic, that the critic of *The Stage* newspaper picked him out from a glittering cast for special praise. No one in the audience, except the director, could have guessed that he had only the vaguest idea of what he was talking about.

At the other extreme is the actor whose approach to his part is primarily intellectual, building up his performance by a searching examination of the motives and feelings behind every thought and action and working out minutely the inflections of voice, gestures and movements to give them expression. The director must meet him on his own ground, agreeing with or disputing the arguments put forward. Having done so, to prevent the eventual performance being arid and lifeless, he must at a suitable moment deliberately disrupt the actor's intellectual flow and force him to bring his instinctive processes into play. They must exist or he would be no actor. Indeed, to talk about a wholly 'intellectual actor' would be a contradiction of terms because the ability to act is an inborn emotional attribute which cannot be acquired. It can be tempered by the mind, but intellect, voice and physique are tools only. All three can be lacking and yet an electrifying performance may occur; all three can be superbly present and make no emotional contact with the audience whatever.

The bad rehearser who is a gifted actor but who is only capable of being so in front of an audience is likely to cause anxious moments for the director, especially if he has not worked with him before. He may apparently waste a great deal of time battling with what appears to be a hopeless case, wondering how he could have been so foolish as to cast him for the part in the first place. The rest of the cast, meanwhile, will almost certainly become intensely irritated by having to rehearse with someone who is walking through his part, giving nothing more than a lifeless repetition of words and drill-like movements. Then on the first night a complete transformation occurs: the near-zombie becomes an actor inspired, holding the audience in the hollow of his hand, at the same time completely throwing the rest of the cast, who find their carefully rehearsed timing and reactions to him no longer relevant. The director, sitting out in front, or more likely pacing up and down with no means of controlling the situation, will certainly be astonished and possibly delighted, depending upon how far the actor's inspiration conforms to what he has been asked to do during those seemingly valueless hours of rehearsal. The chances are that it will. The next time he employs him the director will know the form and be neither unduly anxious nor disheartened by the apparent lack of response at rehearsals. He will moreover warn the cast what to expect. It should be added that nearly all actors 'come up' with an audience, and the director should allow for this. Those who fail to do so have probably been exemplary in rehearsal but, having nothing more to give, their performance will remain exemplary in all things but the one that really matters—emotional contact with the audience.

The ideal actor is one who is full of what the famous director Basil Dean aptly dubbed 'the juice of acting', with the fine intelligence to control it and himself. Of such a kind are the truly great—Laurence Olivier, Sybil Thorndike, John Gielgud, Edith Evans, Paul Schofield, Flora Robson, to name a few in the contemporary English theatre, and on the other side of the Atlantic the Lunts, Helen Hayes, James Stewart, George C. Scott and Walter Matthau. With such, the director will have no problem, provided he knows his job and can make full use of what the gods have given him. What he asks for he will get in superabundance. With experience a director will learn to spot early in rehearsals to what category each of his cast belongs, will apply whatever method seems most appropriate to gain his confidence and co-operation, and will thus eventually achieve a balanced and harmonious overall performance.

In any acting company there is often one dominant figure —for example, the leading actor by long custom in an amateur group or repertory company, or a world-famous star in a London or New York company—who is accustomed to get his own way. Often what he suggests or asks for is helpful or at least can be accepted without harm to the production as a whole. In other instances it may threaten the balance of the scene or even the whole play and must at all costs be resisted. It is here that moral courage may be needed. If argument and persuasion fail to win the day, the director must stand his ground and refuse to be browbeaten. Otherwise he will find that, a breach having been made, a cascade of potentially damaging demands will swamp the well-ordered production he had in mind.

There are certain things which apply to the directing of all actors, regardless of category. Perhaps the most important is to find exactly the right moment in which to feed them an idea. Inexperienced young directors, brimful of ideas and eagerness to express them, too often make the fatal mistake of giving them to the actors before they are ready to receive them. A single idea put into an actor's mind at precisely the right moment may illumine his whole performance. The same idea fed to him before he's ready for it will be totally unproductive. The right moment may be when the actor has gone some way in his own studying of the part. He is reasonably familiar with it but is undecided as to how exactly he is going to play it, or some scene in it, or some individual line. At this moment of indecision, when he is likely to be most receptive, the director pops in his suggestion like a sparrow feeding its young.

The director should be quick to seize upon anything the actor does which is absolutely right for the way he wants the part to be played. Encouragement of the good is likely to prove much more productive than criticism of the bad. The chances are that the former will in time eliminate the need for the latter altogether. It is essential to avoid making an actor feel self-conscious about a particular line or bit of business. It is liable to set up the wrong kind of tension and the actor 'gets a thing about it' which may never quite disappear. This is particularly true about inflections of speech. It is most unwise to 'give an inflection', as such; wrong inflections are almost always due to wrong thinking and, therefore, should be cured by getting the thought right, either by explanation or paraphrase. Putting the thought in different words is often a most useful way of making an actor clear as to the meaning of the line. It must be borne in mind, incidentally, that people have different ways of expressing themselves, and what would be a wrong inflection for one person may be right for another. All that matters is that the thought behind the line is intelligibly expressed.

As with inflection, a gesture should not be given unless it is a definite bit of business such as pointing the way. A good actor will instinctively use his hands naturally as a means of emphasis. An inexperienced actor will become 'hand conscious' if attention is drawn to them except in the most general terms. In fact proper use of the hands and their control is often a chink in the armour of even some experienced professional actors and more often than not completely defeats the amateur beginner. There is no short-term solution, and the director who attempts one only makes matters worse. All he can do is, where possible, find bits of business to keep the offending appendages occupied: hence innumerable smoking of cigarettes, drinking of drinks and, in the case of the ladies, arranging of flowers or clutching of handkerchiefs. In contrast, the late A. E. Matthews, a past master of apparently effortless comedy playing, used his feet as well as his hands, flicking one forward at precisely the right moment as if kicking the line across.

When Bernard Shaw was directing a play he used to demonstrate what he wanted by acting the parts himself with such palpable exaggeration that his intention was abundantly clear but the actors thought to themselves: 'Poor old fool, what a ham! I'll show him how it should be done.' Many fine actors who turn director make the mistake of performing the parts themselves with the intention of the actors copying them. The latter either cannot get anywhere near the dazzling performance which has just been shown them and feel defeated, or they manage a fair imitation which is lifeless because it is superficial, does not come from within themselves, is in fact mimicry rather than true acting. (The same thing often happens when an understudy, who may in fact be a good actor, takes over from a principal.)

In recent years it has become fashionable for some young directors to consider it part of their job to hold 'relaxing exercises' before the rehearsals begin. This is treating the actors as if they were children instead of responsible adults only too well aware that their professional work demands that they keep as fit and alert as possible. How they achieve this is surely up to them individually and not as conscripted members of a physical-training class.

The director should try to make the actor as comfortable and relaxed as possible. He should not keep him waiting about more than necessary and should, therefore, not call him until he needs him (allowing a reasonable margin, of course). He should, except in direct emergency, keep to reasonable hours of rehearsal. If actors are handled with consideration and tact by management and director, and if they gain assurance that the latter knows his job, there are likely to be few so-called 'temperaments'. When they do occur they are usually due to overwrought nerves or over-anxiety. Sometimes they are a cover-up to hide a sudden awareness of ineptitude or a fit of pent-up jealousy. Just occasionally they are plain bad temper. They should be dealt with firmly, perferably by at once seeking out the cause and removing it. If this is not possible, a sharp reproof—a metaphorical slap in the face—may do the trick. A slanging match should be avoided at all costs. If all else fails, it is best to leave the storm to blow itself out. In the theatre, as elsewhere, the proverb 'Let not the sun go down upon thy wrath' is more often than not psychologically wrong. Few outbursts of anger or even silly temperament fail to be assuaged by a good night's sleep.

CHAPTER SEVEN

Rehearsals

DURATION

Opinions will differ widely on the ideal length of time that plays should be rehearsed. Obviously the old weekly repertory system that used to be widespread in England was the reverse of ideal. With matineés intervening, it usually provided no more than twenty-one hours of rehearsal time excluding the dress rehearsal and possibly Sundays, and thus gave little opportunity for director or actors to achieve more than the broad outline of a performance, any subtlety being purely accidental. At the other extreme is the Russian method of rehearsing each play from eight to ten months. Whether such a prolonged period of gestation produces an end-product superior to one by a company of professional English actors of equivalent standing is a matter for debate. Solodovnikov, at one time director of the Moscow Arts Theatre, when asked to comment on such a wide disparity in the length of rehearsal required, once offered the following wholly unlikely explanation: 'Most actors in the West come from a cultural background. In contrast our actors are for the most part peasants.' He elaborated on this theme at some length, with no twinkle in his eye to suggest a leg-pull. More probably it was intended as a gracious compliment to his hosts. Whatever the true explanation, it is likely that any professional English actor subjected to such a rehearsal period would go steadily mad with boredom and frustration.

Most professional repertory companies in England nowadays rehearse for two or three weeks, usually depending upon the length of run of each play. Two weeks is an awkward period. It provides enough time to delve further below the surface than is possible in a week but not enough to develop fully what is found there. Three weeks is a handy time—at its end, with most plays, a production should be just about ready to be presented to an audience for the first time. This does not mean that it will as yet be fully developed. However long a play has been rehearsed, it requires the presence of an audience to bring it to life and to temper it. It will probably require several performances for it to reach its peak. That is the purpose of pre-London and pre-New York tours and their recent equivalents of 'previews at reduced prices'. Although the play will probably have been rehearsed in this case for a month or even longer, it will not be considered ready for an audience paying full metropolitan prices or, perhaps of more vital concern, for the critics, until it is 'run in'.

Most amateur companies suffer the disadvantage of having to prepare their productions over a comparatively long period of short rehearsals, frequently disrupted by the absence of various members of the cast through other demands on their time. According to whatever the rehearsal period available, the director should draw up a carefully considered schedule. Especially in the days of weekly rep, some over-ambitious directors became so engrossed with the first act that they never really got further, so that the last two acts were somehow pushed through by the actors at the dress rehearsal with virtually no direction at all. Even with two or three weeks' rehearsal, the production can easily get out of balance by too much time being spent on certain scenes at the expense of the others. Having a time table and keeping to it fairly strictly will lessen the chance of this happening. It will also be of great value to the actors; they will know what stage in the preparation of their part they will be expected to have reached by any given day, and will plan accordingly. The schedule must, of course, be subject to alteration. Some scenes may prove more difficult than was expected, others less so; actors may be absent through illness or delayed by traffic jams.

Although every director will have his own plan and method of working, depending upon the play, the length of rehearsal period and so forth. It may be of value to give some indication of a possible schedule for, say, a three-weeks' rehearsal of a three-act play. It is assumed that there will be nineteen full working days, with three hours each morning and three hours each afternoon.

First Day	AM	Read through the play and discuss such matters as costumes
	PM	Start plotting moves for Act I
Second Day	AM	Finish plotting Act I
	PM	Start plotting Act II
Third Day	AM	Finish plotting Act II
	PM	Start plotting Act III
Fourth Day	AM	Finish plotting Act III
	PM	Work through entire play without stopping to make sure

F

		that roughly all the movement works
Fifth Day	AM	Rehearse Act I in detail
	PM	Ditto
Sixth Day	AM	Ditto
	PM	Rehearse Act II in detail
Seventh Day	AM	Ditto
	PM	Ditto
Eighth Day	AM	Rehearse Act III in detail
	PM	Ditto
Ninth Day	AM	Ditto
	PM	Run through play without books
Tenth Day		Run through play twice
Eleventh Day		Act I in detail
Twelfth Day		Act II in detail
Thirteenth Day		Act III in detail
Fourteenth Day	AM	Run through
	PM	Act I in detail
Fifteenth Day	AM	Run through
	PM	Act II in detail
Sixteenth Day	AM	Run through
	PM	Act III in detail
Seventeenth Day	AM	Run through, followed by notes
	PM	Ditto
Eighteenth Day	AM	Run through once
Nineteenth Day		Dress Rehearsal

If there are twenty working days, the nineteenth should be used for a technical rehearsal, and the twentieth for the dress rehearsal.

STAGE MANAGEMENT

The smooth running of rehearsals will be greatly helped by efficient stage management and the director should not tolerate anything less. Calls to the actors should be precise, and the stage manager or his assistant must make sure that they are on the spot when required. Rehearsals should start punctually, with the acting area of the scene in question marked out with tape, and furniture and props already set.

The luxury of the actual furniture and props to be used in the production is seldom possible until the last few rehearsals, but adequate substitutes should be there from the start. High standards of prompting should be insisted upon—there are few things more exasperating for an actor still uncertain of his words than not to be prompted when he needs to be—or being prompted unnecessarily when he is making an intentional pause. Whoever is 'on the book' must concentrate his attention on the performance of the actor, making mental notes of where he is likely to dry and when he is deliberately pausing. Curiously enough, when an actor is confident that the person on the book is with him, ready to prompt at exactly the right moment, he is far less likely to dry up. It is also very important that the stage management produces all noise effects—telephones, door slams, etc—bang on cue.

READ-THROUGH

A read-through of the play by the cast as a preliminary to rehearsal is customary if time permits and is valuable from two points of view. It brings the whole company together for the first time and thus provides an early start in the process of creating a corporate feeling. It also provides an opportunity for the director to inform the cast, in broad outline, how he intends to produce the play and how he wants the characters to be interpreted, thus indicating that he has done his prep and knows exactly where he is going: it is the first step in the all-important matter of winning the actors' confidence. If the play is a new one, the author will almost certainly be present and will possibly meet members of the cast for the first time. At the read-through any script changes already agreed between author and director will be given to the actors as they come to them.

It must be said that many actors hate read-throughs—especially those, and there are many such, who though excellent at their job become self-conscious when reading; they stumble over words and feel they are making fools of themselves in front of director, author and brother artists. There are, too, many directors who regard read-throughs as a complete waste of time, contending that all the positive points they achieve can just as easily be made at a 'working rehearsal'. In contrast, it is said that the Russians spend the first three weeks of the eight months' preparation for a production sitting round a table and discussing the play and its characters.

PLOTTING

The next stage of rehearsal is what used to be called 'plotting' but with the coming of TV now tends to be known as 'blocking'. It is the process of working out the movement of the actors. It will be subject to revision as the production develops and new ideas become apparent, but this early rather tedious work is very important as it provides the foundation of the visual structure of the performance.

Directors set about the task in various ways. Some spend many hours before rehearsals begin working out every move in the model of the set, using pins or chessmen to represent the characters. Others prefer to visualise the general action of the play in their mind's eye, marking only major moves and groupings in their scripts, and working out the remaining moves with the actors during rehearsal. The first method establishes a fairly rigid initial structure, saves much time in the early rehearsals, and, provided the director adjusts it as rehearsals proceed and the production develops, will probably end up with much the same answer as the director who, by being flexible to start with, takes more time in the early rehearsals but has to spend less time later on making changes. Whatever the method used, the various functions of movement remain the same. These are:

1. By giving visual variety to attract and hold an audience's attention. A totally static scene (though it can on occasion be used with great effect) tends to make an audience lose concentration. In general terms, an audience should be given the opportunity to see the actors 'three-dimensionally'; that is, at different times during a scene it should be presented with each profile, front-face and back—a kind of concealed mannequin parade. This is automatically achieved in theatre in the round, an advantage which that method has over a proscenium or open-ended stage.

2. To be a primary means of punctuating and accentuating the performance. Here one comes back to the analogy between the director and the conductor of an orchestra. Each must find the right tempo and emphasis to give shape and colour to the play or symphony so that it may have the right impact upon the audience. In the case of the conductor, these things can only be achieved by variations of sound. The director also has movement at his command.

3. To be visually satisfying.

4. To relate the actors to each other and to the audience in the most advantageous way possible to put the play across.

There are certain basic considerations which should be observed unless there is a very good reason for ignoring them.

1. The most commanding position is upstage centre. From here, the actor's front face and, if he merely turns his head,

both profiles are in full view of the entire audience. His voice will be travelling to the audience in a straight line without being impeded.

2. For similar reasons, in placing one actor in relation to another, the upstage position is usually the more favourable one.

3. As an extension of this principle, it will usually be found that the most workable patterns into which to move three or more actors are triangles, with the actor requiring the most prominence at the apex, the base being the imaginary line between the two actors or two groups of actors nearest the audience.

4. An actor with his back to the audience is deprived of his most obviously expressive features (face, eyes and mouth), is speaking away from the audience and must, therefore, greatly raise his voice to be heard.

5. It is usually helpful to place an actor so that his face is turned at least three-quarters to the majority of the audience.

6. An actor standing between another actor and any person in the audience masks him from that person. Similarly an actor passing behind another actor is momentarily obscured from the audience and anything he may be saying is probably rendered inaudible.

7. Three or more actors standing in a straight line look ridiculous and totally unnatural, except for drill or choir practice.

8. Wherever possible an actor should 'move on a line', that is as he is speaking a line, or visually expressing a thought or emotion, giving the impression that the move has been impelled by that thought or emotion, so that he reaches his new position naturally with no suggestion of technical motivation. As it is made at a time when the audience's attention is automatically on him, there is no possibility of it

distracting from any other actor's speech. In the theatre, unike TV or the cinema. it is not usually necessary to be too precise as to the exact spot at which he will land up, thus allowing for a certain amount of flexibility to match length and pace of move to delivery of the line. For example, the instruction 'cross down left to below the chair' allows more ground for a manœuvre than 'cross to chalk mark A', which the exigencies of the camera may demand. The line or expression of thought on which he is to move is probably one to which the director wishes to give emphasis; indeed, to get full value from the use of movement as a means of accentuation, its employment without a particular purpose should be avoided as much as possible.

9. Nevertheless, within the general pattern of movement worked out by the director, the actor should be free to suggest any moves which he feels would be helpful to his performance. There is a story that after Ellen Terry had at rehearsal carried out precisely every one of the meticulous moves given her by the director, Dion Boucicault, she said sweetly: 'And now, Mr Boucicault, I presume you wish me to put in that extra little bit of magic for which you are paying me so much.'

10. In a scene with a great number of people on the stage with little or nothing to say, their movement should be in the form of reactions to what is being said by the principals in the scene, so that, again, it will not distract, and may even emphasise. One can conceive of friends, Romans, and countrymen packed up-stage with full faces to the audience lending their ears to an Antony right down on the edge of the stage where the footlights used to be. Doubtless, it has in fact been done; but to come off successfully it would require a Mark Antony of exceptional vocal strength and eloquent posture, and a crowd of more than average acting ability and dis-

cipline. Few directors would be fortunate enough to have both or even either.

Movement will be governed to a considerable extent by the 'practicalities' of the set, the position and nature of which, it will be remembered, were decided at an early stage in consultation with the designer, and by the furniture, defining that word in general terms to cover all types of production as 'articles upon which people sit, lie down, stand, lean and deposit things'. The placing of the furniture will, in fact, be related by the director to the general pattern of movement he has in mind. He may well change it in the light of experience as the production develops. The degree to which he will be able effectively to change his mind about the practicalities of the set will depend upon when the new thought strikes him, how elaborate the set is, where it is being built and painted, and how much authority he has over those responsible for providing it. The director in a self-contained producing theatre, with its own scenery staff and workshop on the premises, has a great advantage over one who is dependent upon outside contractors. Nevertheless, even in the most favourable circumstances, once the model has been made, material has been measured up and construction started, any structural changes to a set other than minor adjustments should be avoided unless absolutely necessary.

Once the preliminary movement has been worked out, which should take about four days, everybody sighs with relief and the work in detail on each scene begins. This is, from the director's point of view, the heart of the matter, and it is during this middle period of roughly ten days, that he makes his main contribution to the production. It is the time when the author's original play, the actors' interpretative instincts and his own creative imagination are in the melting pot, and from them he beats out an alloy which is itself a new creation, as true and as valid, he hopes, as any of the three elements of which it is composed. As the actors become progressively more familiar with their parts, he seizes on and embellishes what is good in their own interpretation and persuades them to discard what is out of line with the overall performance he is aiming to achieve. At appropriate moments he will be bringing to bear his own suggestions and definite requirements. He should welcome and be ready to consider any promising suggestion from anyone, if he uses it gratefully acknowledging the source. There used to be a type of authoritarian director—there may still be—who resented any suggestion that all the bright ideas in a production were not his own. When anyone dared to put one forward, it was either ignored or dismissed; a day or two later it was likely to turn up as the director's own. Such childish dishonesty fooled no one and created bad feeling, resentment and a mild contempt towards him among the whole company.

The best ideas are often sparked off in discussion. An actor or the director has a small brainwave, the other enlarges upon it, someone else chips in and suddenly a laugh or moment of tension is born in the play. Any director who thinks he has a monopoly of ideas is a fool. What he must do—and this will show his quality as a director—is to judge rightly whether a particular idea from any source contributes or detracts from the production as it is developing.

It is at this stage that the director begins to orchestrate the performance—again the analogy with a conductor creeps in. Both must blend the various individual performances into a harmonious and balanced whole. As too much brass may drown the strings, so too much power from one actor may overwhelm the other participants in a scene. The director— like the conductor—must be continually searching for the 'bumps', the points of emphasis. Some are self-evident; others, the more subtle ones which will eventually give the production its texture, may not reveal themselves until quite late in rehearsals. They are attained by modulations of voice, variations of pace, movement and gesture.

In order that the production should steadily develop, it is important that during this formative period there should be constant consolidation as well as progression. The director should keep a clear distinction, known to the actors, between 'working rehearsals' and 'non-interrupting rehearsals'. At the former he is positively directing, stopping to deal with each point as it arises. At the latter, the actors can concentrate entirely upon their performances (whatever stage these may have reached) without either being stopped by the director or being inhibited by a subconscious expectation of this happening.

A practical and very rewarding method of rehearsing at this stage is to allot to each period a section of the play of a length that enables it to be rehearsed three times: first, 'non-interrupting', then 'working', and finally 'non-interrupting' again. The first acts as a pipe opener and warm-up for the actors, bringing their minds to bear upon the scene in hand, and exercises their memories in finding the words and their vocal organs in formulating them. During it the director watches intently, making mental notes on what needs correction, what needs developing and how this is to be done, what should be mentioned now and what left until a later day. Thus actors and director are able to assess from each of their points of view how far the production has progressed.

During the 'working' rehearsal, the scene is taken to pieces—like a suit after a fitting by the tailor. The director says what he has to say as each point is reached. The actors bring up any suggestions they wish to make or anything about which they are worried or uncertain. Between them they thrash out a mutually acceptable answer. Every change or addition is rehearsed several times until it fits comfortably into the scene.

The final 'non-interrupting' rehearsal consolidates in the actors' minds what has been done. The director may give notes at the end, but they should only be obvious ones dealing with that day's work and no more than can be rehearsed there and then. Any new ideas or changes that have occurred to him should be reserved until the next time the scene comes up on the schedule.

On the subject of giving notes, there is a considerable difference of practice among directors. Some hold very strongly that commonsense and any knowledge of the process of acting indicates that a note to an actor should be rehearsed, if only once, at the time it is given. A change of move should be walked through; a change of emphasis spoken within its context. Otherwise, the next time the actor goes through the scene, he will probably do a kind of mental hiccough as his brain signals to him that he had a note to do something or other at this juncture. Even if he remembers what it was, his performance will have temporarily lost its rhythm. If he does not, it was a waste of time giving it to him. Some directors—even some very good ones—evidently have not considered the matter or choose to disregard the argument. They shower notes upon their actors like confetti with no attempt whatever to rehearse them. They often choose the most seemingly unsuitable moments to do so—such as after the final dress rehearsal, or even immediately before the first performance when most actors are strung up with nerves and at their least receptive.

As these directors seem to get away with it without apparent serious damage to their productions, they may be right in deciding that it is easy to exaggerate the sensitivity of an actor's mind. When Bernard Shaw was directing a play, he used to sit in the auditorium during a 'non-interrupting' rehearsal, taking notes by the light of a torch which he turned on as required. One can imagine few things more disconcerting to an actor concentrating on his performance than to have signalled to him the fact that the director is making a note—he presumes about him. Yet, as far as is known, no actor walked out in consequence. Nevertheless, such distraction is surely undesirable, to say the least, and can be avoided. If there is not sufficient light reflected from the stage or from exit signs or secondary lighting for the director to make his notes in a reasonably legible scrawl—and there usually is—any special light for his purpose should be kept on throughout the rehearsal and his notebook not be so close to it that its use is seen from the stage.

It is suggested in the schedule that the final stages of rehearsals should be a series of run-throughs of the whole play followed by detailed work each day on a single act. By now the production should have taken its rough shape—in some ways like a diamond that has just been cut; all that remains is to smooth and polish each facet until it finally contributes its individual sparkle to the brilliance of the whole. But a diamond, however much it glitters, remains static and inanimate. The performance of a play is a living thing, with all the variations and mutation of an organism constantly renewing itself. It has rhythm and pace; it has mood. It is these things which the director will be watching for, especially during these final run-throughs, together with the pitch of the actors' voices both in relation to each other and to the eventual audience. He will also be looking out for bits of business which need tidying up, for any awkward moves which may have persisted and can be eased; in fact, subtle changes of any kind which will add to the texture of the production. He should watch from different parts of the auditorium and, so far as it is possible for any-one so closely involved, put himself in what will be the audience's place, asking himself searching questions. Is the play coming across as he intended? Is its meaning clear? Does it hold one's interest all through? Are the actors audible? (Words unheard might just as well not be spoken.) If the answer to any of these questions is 'no' he must, of course, do all he can to remedy the situation. He must at the same time judge whether the value of any change that seems desirable will be outweighed by the upset it may cause.

It would be extraordinary if he were satisfied with every-thing as he sees it at the final run-through. However, there comes a time—and this is it—when his main preoccupation will be with physical and technical matters rather than the text and its interpretation.

CHAPTER EIGHT

Dfess Rehearsal

The climax of rehearsals, when all the various elements of a production—performance, scenery, costumes, lighting, music and sound effects—come together for the first time, is usually referred to as 'the production period'. The method employed to bring about this vital synthesis will depend upon the size and nature of the production and to some extent upon the time and facilities available. A big musical will require a different method and much more time than a single set comedy. It is proposed here to discuss straight plays which do not require elaborate staging—the kind of play, in fact, with which repertory companies and amateur groups are mostly concerned.

The first consideration is time: how much is needed and how much is available. The answer to the first question is ideally three days (the third probably being the day of the first performance). But many repertory companies which close on a Saturday night with one production and open on the following Monday with another have cheerfully to content themselves with staging the set or sets on the

Sunday, dressing and lighting them on Monday morning, and dress rehearsing the play, possibly with the taking of display photographs included, on Monday afternoon.

The advantages of an extra day, if this is at all possible, are many. It takes some of the pressure off everybody concerned. It allows a reasonable margin for hitches and minor crises and therefore more chance of reaching the deadline without panic. It provides an opportunity for meticulous lighting, the department which tends to suffer most when time is short. It enables the actors to have the boon of two dress rehearsals—the first slow and primarily technical, stopping as the need arises, and the second non-interrupting.

Whatever the time available, there are certain highly desirable if not essential requirements if the operation is to go smoothly. First, efficient stage management is even more important at this stage than it has been during preliminary rehearsals. Although the duties and functions of the stage-management staff are not strictly speaking the concern of the director, except in so far as they succeed or fail in providing him with what he wants, he depends upon them to such an extent that it is appropriate that they should be stated here.

1. The organisation and control of all activity back-stage. In particular the control of the stage staff—carpenters, electricians and property men—and their instruction beforehand as to precisely what each is to do throughout the performance, especially if there are any scene changes.

2. Supervising the setting up of scenery, and the placing and marking of all furniture and properties (after the position has been decided by the director and, in the case of decoration, by the designer).

3. Giving cues from the prompt corner to the flyman to

raise or drop the curtain, to the electrician for light changes, and for all sound effects, either taped or mechanical.

4. Maintaining discipline back-stage. This covers such things as general behaviour, arriving for the peformance at an appointed time (usually half an hour before curtain rise), talking or smoking in the wings, missing entrances, getting in the way during scene changes, fooling on stage, being drunk and so forth. In most professional companies the disciplinary powers which the stage manager's job bestows rarely have to be invoked.

5. Backing up the actor—in many ways the most important part of the stage manager's job. It should be an attitude of mind which, when present, infuses many routine matters with a sense of purpose and professional pride, even dedication. Actors should be able to feel as much confidence in the stage management as racing drivers do in the mechanics in the pits. In practice, it is gained by the sum total of many things; for example, the stage management should ensure (*a*) the actors' creature comforts, by such things as seeing that the dressing-rooms have their full complement of chairs and electric light bulbs, that the basins are clean and not blocked up, that there are chairs in the wings for them to sit on while waiting to go on stage; (*b*) that the actors receive correct calls and are informed of any changes of plan. This is particularly important as dress rehearsals very seldom start on time and the less actors are kept waiting about the better; (*c*) that all hand props are either handed to the actor or are in a position off-stage known to the actor; (*d*) that all sound and off-stage effects are timed by *feeling* the actor's performance; (*e*) that an actor is prompted when he needs to be and not otherwise. The art of prompting, which every stage manager should study, lies in closely linking in one's mind the words one is reading

in the text with the rhythm with which the actor is speaking them. In this way one can sense a 'dry' as it happens and feed the actor with the missing words without a perceptible pause. They should be given clearly but not louder than is necessary for the actor to hear.

This particular matter is stressed because in the professional theatre the standard of stage management has dropped in recent years, chiefly because the TV companies have offered much more lucrative and in some ways less onerous jobs to anyone with a year or two's experience in the theatre. Consequently, just as a member of the stage management begins to show real signs of knowing his job, he departs for the television studios. Whereas, before the coming of television, a director could take the efficiency of the stage management more or less for granted, he must be ready nowadays to crack a whip to get what he wants.

The next most desirable requirement for a smooth operation is an efficient and keen stage crew—that is carpenter, electrician, property master (if any) and their respective assistants. If the carpenter and his assistants have constructed the scenery themselves, they will know where each piece goes and how it is fitted together. There should, therefore, be no unnecessary delay in setting it up provided that they have done all possible preparatory work and that such things as cleats, cleat lines, pin-hinges, hanging irons, french braces, castor wheels, all catches and other essential pieces of equipment are already in position on each relevant piece of scenery.

The electrics staff usually have the most time-consuming work to do and therefore are liable to cause most delays, especially if they have failed to do all possible preparatory work, such as having all necessary equipment properly wired up and in working order, and colour filters cut and framed, with spares of varying colours handy in case of changes of mind. The speed at which the setting up and positioning of lighting equipment is carried out will vary greatly according to the facilities available. If the theatre is a modern one with catwalks on a level with the lanterns, the electrician can put in a filter of the required colour and focus and point each lantern to the area it is to light in a matter of a minute or two and pass quickly on to the next one. In many theatres, however, he still has to climb a tall ladder which must be shifted for every one or at most two lanterns. As furniture and sometimes scenery has to be moved to make way for it and other departments on the stage are interrupted in their work, it is usually advisable, if time permits, to allot a definite and adequate period after the sets have been erected to nothing but fixing the lighting.

The duties of the property department have in recent years been taken over in many theatres by the junior members of the stage-management staff. Again, whoever is responsible for them must be sure that everything required is ready in time and in position. To ensure that nothing is missing, each item should be checked against a list—'the property list'—which should incidentally be used at every performance of the run of a play.

Next to preparation, patience is the most important factor contributing to things going smoothly. Everything tends to take longer than one bargained for, and little unexpected snags tend to hold things up. Expression of impatience or loss of temper may not only rattle the staff, who are probably doing their damnedest, and thus delay things still further, but are wearing on the nerves.

In the early stages of the production period, the function of the director is primarily to supervise and to be the ultimate authority to whom any matter requiring a decision should be referred. It is important that he should be present when the set or sets are erected and dressed. Although the set is the designer's responsibility, the director may wish to make some alteration, perhaps because of sight lines (particularly if they were designed without the production theatre in mind) or the position of the light bars, or even because in full size a minor alteration would improve upon the model. All 'dressing' (that is, props which are purely decoration) is, again, the designer's responsibility, but if the director disapproves of any item he will request its removal. The positioning of the furniture is the director's responsibility. It should be marked by the stage management, generally with coloured adhesive tape.

The next stage is lighting the set, either by the director or a specialist. A special chapter deals with this very important operation. Should it be done by a specialist, it will obviously be in close consultation with the director, who again must have the last word should there be any disagreement.

The actors first meet the set at the technical rehearsal (if there is time for one). The usual practice is to go right through the play solely for the purpose of making sure that everything works, of adjusting the timing of moves, of possibly rearranging the grouping to conform to the lines of sight and rehearsing any business which is affected by the scenery. All sound effects, including any recorded background music, should have been tried out during the last week, at least, of rehearsals. However, it may well be necessary to adjust the volume of the amplifiers to take into account the set and the size of the theatre. A warning here— a theatre full of people acts as a damper on sound, and therefore volumes should be set well above what seems right when the theatre is empty.

During the 'technical', if the lighting has already been plotted, it is valuable to try it out with the actors present and making their moves. This may well show the need for adjustment—a change of light strength here, the repositioning of a spot there.

With all this the director is as actively and positively involved as he has been throughout rehearsals. From then on, however, he will delegate much of his authority to the stage manager, who will take full charge once the curtain is up on the dress rehearsal—the final non-interrupter, 'as on the night'. The director should in no way interfere with him nor set foot on stage, unless asked to do so, even if the rehearsal grinds to a halt because of some hitch. He should be out in front making notes, primarily of technical matters: is the lighting now right? On consideration, is the position of the furniture as favourable to the actors as it could be? Do any of the clothes need altering? Does some piece of stage dressing blur the faces of actors playing in front of it? Once more he is being a kind of precursor of the audience, this time concerned hardly at all with the actors' performances but with sheer mechanics. The performances will in any case not be worth critically considering. The actors will be too unrelaxed, too preoccupied adjusting themselves to their clothes and the set to give anything like of their best.

A director may comfort himself with the knowledge that a bad dress rehearsal often augurs well for the first night. The actors and staff tend to react against their depression over the way things have gone by giving an exceptionally fine performance. Managers have even been known to induce the depression in order to get the required reaction. The late Henry Sherek, who presented a revival of *His House in Order* in 1951, went to each dressing-room in turn after what had been a reasonably good dress rehearsal, telling the occupants how bad they were. When the director, incredulous and infuriated, asked what the hell he thought he was doing, destroying in a few minutes the confidence which he, the director, had spent several weeks building up, Sherek replied: 'Cochran taught me that trick. Get the company furious with you and they'll go on to the stage with guns fully blazing just to show you how wrong you were.' Such draconian methods might be effective in rousing an apathetic or over-complacent company, but their necessity is questionable if the director has done his job properly.

First-night nerves are a professional affliction which few actors are lucky enough to escape. The experienced director knows they are not cured by forced heartiness or over-emphatic reassurances. They are aggravated rather than allayed by last-minute notes. If the director is wise, therefore, he will keep his courtesy visit to the dressing-room as brief as possible, and say little more than wish the actor luck. He should in any case be careful not to make any remark which the latter, in his apprehension, may misunderstand. It could have disastrous results. For example, on one occasion, a charming but inexperienced manager, doing the rounds before an important London first night, happened to remark to the young leading man that the theatre, although larger than he would have wished, had exceptionally good acoustics, and thus luckily did not demand any unusual strength of voice. After he had gone, the actor panicked, thinking that, 'he is hinting to me in the nicest possible way that I was using far too much voice at the dress rehearsal'. The result was a performance so muted that it could hardly be heard. The rest of the company tended to come down to the same level and by the end of the first act the audience's interest was completely lost and the production doomed.

Good or bad, the first performance will provide many answers which neither director nor actors, however skilled and experienced, could be sure about until the production is played to an audience. The relationship between actor and audience has a very positive quality. It is a kind of emotional alternating current which, flowing back and forth between the two, conditions on the one hand the actor's performance and on the other the audience's reaction to it.

The director is, of course, not directly involved in this relationship. He can only observe its outcome and this he must do carefully and analytically, so that he may adjust and, at his discretion, reshape his production in the light of what the performance has revealed. Where and why did the tension drop and the audience's interest flag? What scenes need cutting or building up? Which lines have, in action, become spare and should be cut because the audience gets the idea without them? Why has an expected laugh failed to come? What has provoked an unexpected and possibly unwanted laugh? These and similar questions he will try to resolve by constructive comments to the actors.

It does not usually take many performances before a production assumes its final shape and rhythm. It is a remaining responsibility of the director to see that these are maintained throughout the run of the play.

CHAPTER NINE

Lighting the Production

Until comparatively recently responsibility for lighting a production was automatically accepted as being that of the director. His primary concern was with the lanterns—spotlights, floods, footlights and the rest—which lit the actors and the set; their position, the area upon which they were focused, their intensity and colour. The control of the electric current which fed them was the responsibility of the electrician and it was not necessary for the director to know more about it than the functional limitations imposed by the nature of the switchboard and the current-bearing capacity of each circuit.

With the development of much more sophisticated methods of control and consequent increase in the number of dimmer circuits available, making possible a great proliferation of lanterns, the job of lighting, both planning and executing, now takes up more time than a director can afford to give to any one element in his production. Especially during the production period, it is highly desirable that he should be free to concentrate on the blending process rather than on the details of its constituents. Thus it has become normal practice in most professional productions for lighting to be delegated by the director to a 'lighting designer'. In repertory companies he will most likely be the chief electrician or the production manager, or possibly an assistant director; in amateur companies some enthusiastic non-acting member of the group with the necessary technical qualifications. In London or New York he will almost certainly be a specialist in the literal sense of the word—a man (or woman —the late Jean Rosenthal in New York is generally acknowledged to be the greatest we have yet seen) who is not only expertly acquainted with the potentialities and limitations of every kind of switchboard and piece of apparatus extant, but has studied in depth the qualities and aesthetic values of applied light. In other words, something of an engineer but even more of an artist.

Whatever his professional status, the lighting designer has much the same relationship to the director as the scene designer has: he is the expert to plan, advise and ultimately execute, but always in conformity with the director's requirements and wishes. He must, of course, also work in close association with the scene designer, in order to stake a claim for positioning his lanterns and to ensure as far as possible that his lighting enhances the effectiveness of the design.

Even if the director does not do his own lighting, it is very desirable that he should know enough about the subject to be able to discuss it, to express his wishes or make his comments about it with authority and in terms which the designer fully understands. The rest of this chapter is intended to provide that amount of knowledge. There are two excellent books by specialists given in the bibliography on page 131 which should be read by anyone wishing to study the subject in depth.

It has already been stated that the director—and the lighting designer—is mainly concerned with the lanterns: the sources of light. These, in various types and sizes, may be grouped in three main categories; spotlights, floods and projectors.

Spotlights focus light by means of a lens upon a selected area of the stage. Though early types of doubtful efficiency can still be met with, those in general use are of two kinds: profile spots (US Lekolites), which provide an even overall beam that can be shaped by shutters or metal masks and given either a hard or soft focus by the lens; and fresnel spots (US Fresnelites), which through a 'stepped' lens give a soft-edged beam. Both kinds are of 500W, 1,000W or 2,000W.

Floods, having no lens, give a spread light, the area covered usually being determined by the nature of the beam thrown by the reflector. Open floods (US Olivettes), with wide-beam reflectors giving maximum spread and with 500W or 1,000W lamps, are used for lighting backcloths, backings and cycloramas, and to provide soft light to fill in areas unlit by spotlights. Although unfortunately no longer manufactured in England, a family of floods with powerful narrow beams thrown by silvered-glass reflectors, called 'acting areas' and 'pageants', are still in use in many theatres. They are invaluable for cutting through other lighting—for example, imitating the rays of the sun. Compartment battens and footlights are small floods joined together in lengths, each with its reflector, low-powered lamp (usually 150W or 200W) and colour slide, and usually wired alternately in three or four circuits. Before the development of spotlights, battens were the main source or even the only source of overhead lighting, but nowadays are usually relegated to lighting backcloths or providing 'fill-in' light.

Footlights (or floats as they are usually called in England

—a relic of the days when they were lighted wicks floating in troughs of melted tallow) stretch across the front edge of the stage. At one time they complemented battens as a principal source of light. Nowadays, when spotlights from the auditorium are used to light the actor at the front of the stage much more effectively and from a less unnatural angle, their chief function is to eliminate any remaining shadows cast by hat, eye sockets, nose or chin. Occasionally, at a subdued level, they may be used to colourtone the setting.

Projectors are of two kinds: an optically simple one taking a 1,000W or 2,000W lamp, which is used with effect machines for producing moving shadow-graphs of various kinds—clouds, waterfalls, waves, snow, etc—and a much more precise instrument, taking 4,000W or 5,000W lamps, for projecting scenery.

Fortunately for any director whose aptitudes do not include a ready understanding of electronic engineering and technique, the nature and functions of stage lanterns have remained fairly simple and straightforward. It is far otherwise with the methods of controlling the electric current which feeds them. However, provided that the light from each lamp can be increased, decreased or extinguished at his command it matters little to him whether this is achieved with a 'pot' dimmer made out of a drain pipe and brake drums, a slider dimmer, a rotary dimmer, a transformer dimmer, a saturated reactor dimmer, a thryratron or a thyristor. Nor need it concern him (except in terms of time and patience) whether the electrician in charge operates them by tugging a string, pulling a lever, presetting them with organ keys or pushing a button to jog a computer's memory. He will quickly learn from experience and from the comments of his electrician the potentialities and limitations of the particular system in use, and will plan his lighting plot accordingly.

What he must familiarise himself with are the colours available for use in the lanterns; these will play an important part in achieving the quality of light he has visualised. The filters mostly used are sheets of dyed plastic with the trade name in England of Cinemoid and in America Roscolene. There are approximately sixty different shades. In view of the imprecise nature of stage lighting one cannot help thinking that, for example, the difference between 'chocolate-tint' and 'pale chocolate' is an over-refinement born of specialist enthusiasm, unlikely to make any discernible contribution to the effectiveness of the stage picture. Even among specialists the number would seem to be excessive. A well-known lighting designer's published plots for five major productions show that he used a total of no more than twenty-four different colours. He could probably have achieved much the same effect without nine of these. It may be argued that, with so many filters to choose from, there is no point in restricting oneself to fifteen : none perhaps, except that in so inexact a process as lighting a three-dimensional stage picture containing any number of colours reflected from varying textures in the scenery, furniture and costumes, and with lamp filaments which change colour at different dimming levels, it is a waste of time to ponder whether to use a 17 steel blue or a 67 steel tint.

Because the lighting process is so imprecise and there is by the nature of things so little time during the production period to make the adjustments which will inevitably be required, it is all the more important that every detail should as far as possible be planned in advance. Certain simple rules and methods must be constantly borne in mind.

Lighting has three objectives. First—and very much foremost—to illuminate the actor; second, to make visible and, where opportune, enhance the set; third, to contribute to the creation of the right mood for each scene. The designer must plan to position his lanterns—'rigging', it is called—so that they can most effectively carry out these functions. His decisions will in a large part be governed by the nature and the architecture of the building, the positions of the circuit terminals, the number and type of lanterns and controls at his disposal, and the structure of the set. Conditions may vary from a village hall with a dozen or so circuits (without dimmers), feeding battens, floats and perhaps half a dozen spots, to a modern metropolitan theatre with facilities for controlling three hundred lanterns placed wherever required in front of or behind the proscenium arch. To discuss them all in detail would require more space than a single chapter. Fortunately, the rules for good lighting are in all essentials much the same whatever the conditions, the principal difference being the number of lanterns used.

Since the lighting of the actors must, except on rare occasions, be an absolute first priority, it follows that the acting area—the part of the stage on which they perform—should be given a basic illumination which will ensure that their features, especially their eyes, can be clearly seen from all parts of the auditorium. As the face consists of a number of bumps, cavities and projections which in terms of visibility are made distinctive from each other by varying degrees of light and shadow, it is important that light from the lanterns should reach the face at an angle which will show its contours to the best advantage. Eye-level frontal lighting will tend to flatten the contours, low-level lighting will cause them to appear unnatural (since daylight comes from above). Near-perpendicular high-level lighting will cause deep unnatural shadows, especially in the eye sockets, and in doing so will obscure the eyes. These sockets, as it happens, hold the key to the problem—they are usually at an angle of about 45° to the face and therefore it is at about this angle that the beam from the lantern should reach the face. Like so many other aspects of stage lighting, this cannot be precise—for one thing the angle will inevitably change as the actor moves around—but it is a useful rule-of-thumb. Carrying it a stage further, the aim is to have beams of light reaching either side of the actor's face at an angle of approximately 45° wherever in the acting area he happens to be.

The most practical way of planning this is to divide the stage into areas of a size that a spotlight beam can fill at the 'throw' available. Into each area two spots are focused, one from each side and from a position in the auditorium, or from the lighting bar immediately behind the proscenium, which will reach the actor's face at something near the magic 45°. By overlapping the edges of the spots in one area with those in the next, and by 'filling in' with extra spotlights or with floods, both sides of the actor's face will be properly lit as he moves anywhere on the stage.

Apart from the lighting from the auditorium—most valuable for taking care of downstage areas—and the lighting from immediately behind the proscenium, valuable positions for providing lighting on the actors are from the side. Here the lanterns are clamped to vertical pipes secured to the ground (called booms) or suspended from the flies and called ladders. To avoid over-lighting in close proximity, or throwing shadows from one actor's face on to another's, boom lanterns should usually be mounted well above head height.

If the set permits, the actor can be made to stand out completely from his background by back-lighting with spotlights facing downstage from a bar at the back of the set and masked from the audience. He may also, of course, be lit by spotlights shining through windows or other special sources. But these are all supplementary to the basic area illumination.

Which type of spotlight will be used in each position may well depend upon what is available. It must be borne in mind that when the distance between a source of light and the object upon which it falls is doubled, its intensity is decreased by three-quarters. This 'inverse square law' requires that, to achieve a rough balance, the higher-power lamps should be in the positions demanding the longest throw—almost always the Front of House—and that there should be enough of them to cover a given area with comparatively narrow beams giving maximum intensity. They will also almost certainly be profile rather than fresnel as the nature of the latter is to 'scatter' light. On the spotlights and booms behind the proscenium, 500W spots will prove the most useful. Whether they are profile or fresnel will depend upon whether a sharp or a soft focus is required.

Having made certain that the whole acting area can be effectively in light from every angle, the next job is to consider the rigging of 'special' lanterns, to suggest, for example, shafts of sunlight coming through a window (beam lights, pageants or tilted acting areas on stands above head height are the most effective), or to work in conjunction with what are referred to as 'practicals'—lamps, wall brackets, chandeliers, etc. The object here must be to give the impression that the pool of light is coming from the practical, care being taken to avoid throwing a too discernible shadow of it on to the scenery or furniture. Other 'specials' will give concentrated pools of light on to walls or trees or other surfaces to give an impression of sunlight in an outdoor scene, or a view through a window. Some plays call for moments of 'dramatic lighting'—often strong contrast between intense light and heavy shadow—and any 'specials' required for this should be put into position at this stage.

Having thus rigged the lanterns which will provide what might be called the 'functional' lighting, the next thing to decide is if and what additional equipment will be required for decorative purpose, that is, lighting or enhancing the set or helping to create the right mood.

If the setting is backed by a curved cyclorama, this should be lit with floods (not less than 1,000W) placed sufficiently down-stage to give a wide and even spread. It is usual to mask the base of a cyclorama with a ground row or piece of built scenery, and fresnel spots should be rigged on an up-stage spot bar to take care of this. If room permits, it is valuable to have either floods or compartment lengths between the ground row and the cyclorama.

If backcloths are being used, they may be lit by battens at close range or, if greater brightness is required, by 1,000W floods which should hang at least six feet from the cloth in order to avoid shadows from each lantern. As with a cyclorama, fresnel spots should be placed to light any ground row in front of the cloth or highlight any feature or features painted on it. Backings outside windows and doors or behind arches should be lit with floods or fresnel spots (preferably the latter) fixed well above head height to avoid shadows being thrown on the backings by passing actors.

Apart from such peripheral features, it may be taken as a general rule that there should be as little direct light on the scenery as possible. There are three reasons for this. Direct light tends to flatten the painting on two-dimensional scenery and to cast unwanted and unnatural shadows on three-dimensional. Secondly, direct light reflected off the set behind an actor detracts from the lighting on his face, thus neutralising to some extent the effectiveness of the acting-area lighting. Thirdly, there will almost certainly be enough 'bounce' from the latter—reflection from the stage and furniture—to reveal the scenery adequately and without over-emphasising it. If it is decided that some direct light on the set will enhance it, or, by affecting the overall colour-tone, help create an atmosphere appropriate to the scene, it should come from special lanterns, battens or possibly footlights which are independently controlled.

Having planned where and at what angle the lanterns should be placed, the next matter to decide is what colour filter should be used in each of them. Colour plays an important part in stage lighting but it should be used with discretion. It is tempting for any one expert in the science and art of mixing coloured light to seize the chance of using all the resources of a theatre's modern equipment to create marvellously subtle pictorial effects. It is, however, rare that a designer can legitimately indulge himself in 'painting the stage in colour'. His job, as has been said, is primarily to light the actors' faces—and in ninety-nine plays out of a hundred in a way that makes them appear natural. This can be achieved ingeniously and arduously by using a great battery of lanterns with an assortment of different colours and overlapping them to achieve the required mixture. Valuable time will be spent in adjusting the dimmers to give exactly the right degree of intensity for each lantern, and in trying to eradicate the multi-coloured shadows which they will throw. Much more simple and economical is the normal practice of using pale-colour filters which will either 'warm' or 'cool' the so-called white light of a tungsten lamp at full voltage to an acceptably natural tone. Most commonly used for warm tones are cinemoid 52 (pale gold) or 53 (pale salmon), and for cool tones 17 (steel blue) or 18 (light blue).

What filters to use in the rest of the lanterns will obviously depend upon their particular functions. Those used in conjunction with an ostensible light source should suggest the appropriate colour tone of that source—for example, warm yellowish with an oil lamp, possibly 3 (straw). Moonlight is usually represented by one or other of the light blues— 17, 18 or 40; and firelight by 34 (golden amber) or a mixture of 4 (medium amber) and 11 (dark pink).

If a cyclorama is being used as a sky cloth, as it is nine times out of ten, the most practical colours in the floods or batten lighting its upper half are a mixture of light blue (18 or 40) and dark blue (19 or 32). At different levels these will suggest most of the gradations of light to be found in the upper reaches of the sky under most climatic conditions from dawn to sunset. The floods or battens between the ground row and the cyclorama should be coloured light blue (18 or 40), and if a dawn or sunset is called for two special circuits, one of 5A (deep orange) and the other of 16 (blue green), should be added.

The colour with which to light a cloth will depend upon how it has been painted. More often than not the answer is open white. The colours in the fresnels lighting the ground row or built pieces at the base of the cyclorama or backcloth will again depend upon how they are painted or what effect is required. If it has been decided that there should be direct overall light on the set, the colours used must depend upon the tonal values of the painting and, again, upon what effect is required. It should be taken into account that the light is likely to be at a subdued level and that the filament in the lamp will, therefore, be burning at a low voltage and giving a yellowish light.

Whereas the rigging, focusing and colouring of the various lanterns can and should be reasonably accurately planned beforehand, the relative intensity required of each can be no more than guessed at until the lighting rehearsal when the set, furniture and stand-ins for the actors are physical realities. There are too many imponderables: the variations in luminosity caused by the different distances of the lanterns from the area each is lighting and by the possible difference in wear of the filament of each lamp; the imprecise efficiency of mass-produced reflectors and lenses; the reflective properties of the various surfaces; and so forth. Fortunately, with modern lighting-control techniques all such variations can be dealt with and the required intensities obtained quickly and precisely as soon as the designer calls for them.

What those requirements are will usually be governed by certain basic considerations. A more or less uniform level of illumination in a single overall colour would give a totally flat effect, in particular of the actors' features. Therefore, to give depth, interest and texture to the overall picture, and in particular to illuminate the actor three-dimensionally, modelling his features to allow them full expression, the designer used contrasts of light and colour. These he achieves either by using different colour filters or varying the intensities of light coming from lanterns set at opposing angles. In deciding which lantern shall be high key and which low key, he will be guided by the nature of the ostensible source of illumination and the direction from which it is coming.

To take a simple example, if in an interior scene sunlight is coming through a window on the left, the spotlights lighting the left-hand side of the actor's face may contain cinemoid 51 (gold tint), the right-hand side the deeper shade of 52 (pale gold), with the 'fill-in' light of 50 (pale yellow) on the left and possibly 18 (light blue) on the right. If in a following scene the curtains are drawn and the room is being dominantly lit by a standard lamp on the right, the 51s will be dimmed to a level below the intensity being given by the 52s. The designer, with the circuit number of each lantern at the tip of his tongue and a precise knowledge, having planned it, of where each is focused, should be as swift as possible in adjusting their various intensities to the required levels. If he has not finished the job within, say, an hour he will be wise to take a short break to rest his eyes. Otherwise he is likely to lose his sense of intensity values and will almost certainly under-light.

When the Windsor Theatre reopened in 1933 with a large-scale production, the director, who lit it himself, spent sixty-three hours adjusting and readjusting the dimmer levels of a three-circuit compartment batten, three circuits of footlights, six spotlights, six hanging floods and six floor floods on stands—the meagre total equipment of the theatre at that time. When, at long last, the curtain went up on the dress rehearsal, the actors could hardly be seen. As there was no time for any further mucking about, the director was over-ridden and to his fury all lamps were ordered to be full up for the rest of the play.

It must be constantly borne in mind that, at whatever cost to subtlety and pictorial effect, the actors' faces must be visible from all parts of the auditorium unless there is some specific reason why they should not be. In other words, the low-key acting-area lights must not drop below an acceptable level. This is the one thing above all that the director must insist upon.

It would indeed be unwise to remind oneself, except when mistakes occur, that audiences generally expect that what they see is intended and satisfy themselves with their own explanations of sometimes the oddest happenings. In a play called *Little Holiday* dealing with the illegal entry of Jews into Palestine during the late 1940s, a three-tier truck, representing a cross-section of the decks of a hell ship, was rolled down-stage in a blackout to a very precise mark. The scene which followed was lit by a single 500W spot on the No 1 Bar focused on two actors lying on the centre 'deck'. On the first night the truck was pushed too far, with the result that the light from the spot shone brightly on the corpse-like face of a dummy on the top deck. A guest of the author's wife, presumably in search of symbolism, was most impressed: 'That shows he's a genius. Most directors would have lit the actors.'

CHAPTER TEN

Budgeting

Apart from the status of the actors, the acquired skills and the amount of time involved, the most obvious distinction between professional and amateur productions is the degree to which basic decisions are related to finance. Artists' salaries, the fees of producer, director and designer and the wage bill of those in support, from stage manager to box-office clerk, will probably represent at least half the cost of mounting a professional production, and will not occur at all in the case of an amateur one.

Even so, any but the most elementary production by an amateur group must involve money and necessitate the keeping of accounts. Whether professional or amateur, it is important, if financial chaos is not to ensue, that a production should be properly budgeted before it is set in motion: that is to say that its estimated cost should be related to the probable money available to pay it.

The extent to which the director will be concerned in this will depend upon his position in the organisation which is presenting the play. If he is boss of a professional company, responsible for its finances as well as the direction of its productions, he will, of course, work out the budget himself. If he is responsible to an administrator or a committee, he may still do so but will probably either be given an overall upper limit or will submit what he regards as his requirement for approval. Even if he is in no way responsible for the financial arrangements, he should be informed of the general budgetary plan and thus be able to visualise the scale of his production. To think big and find there are not the means to implement one's ideas is as frustrating as to find that one has been thinking small unnecessarily.

Whoever draws up the budget can approach the task from either of two diametrically opposed directions. One is to decide how much the play would cost if produced to a particular standard and then find the means to cover that cost— at least on paper. The other is to estimate how much money is likely to be available and apply this sum to the production, alloting so much to each item of expenditure.

The 'cost first and finance afterwards' approach is likely to be practised only by managers presenting individual professional productions in London or New York or on tour. If they are prudent, they will estimate their production costs generously to allow for the unpredictable, and in deciding on the capital required will include a sufficient sum to subsidise running costs over a reasonable period. Many potentially successful shows have failed through lack of cash to nurse them through the early stages of the run before they have had time to become established. Such under-capitalisation is often due to a misguided attempt by the manager to limit the number of shares on which dividends will be paid in the event of a success. The other danger that the 'cost first, finance afterwards' manager must be careful to avoid is putting the play into a theatre which lacks the financial capacity to cover costs. Some years ago, there was a notorious case of a musical which ran for many months in London to capacity, but lost heavily every week. The manager who presented it went bankrupt.

For the most part, directors will be concerned with budgets in which the overall costs must be kept within a predetermined sum. In the case of an unsubsidised project, this is usually based upon the financial capacity of the auditorium in which the play is to be presented. An estimate is then made of what percentage of that capacity the play in question is likely to take at the box-office during its run (ancillary revenue from programmes and bars may be thrown in for good measure), and the costs kept below this figure. In a professional repertory company, presenting a continuous succession of plays, estimates of takings will probably be made of a group of productions, and the budget for each one will not necessarily keep within its individual estimated earning power. Profits from plays which are relatively cheap or expected to be exceptionally popular will be set against losses from plays which are expensive or likely to have limited appeal. In the case of subsidised companies, the 'unearned increment' may be regarded as profit and a similar balance struck between productions.

To estimate with reasonable accuracy the percentage of capacity a particular play will earn—in other words, how many people are going to pay to see it—is the most difficult job facing a theatrical manager. The solvency of his company will depend upon his ability to judge correctly more frequently than not—unless, of course, it is receiving sufficient subsidies to compensate for ineptitude. Whatever the figure estimated and the consequent upper limit of expenditure decided upon, it is imperative that the producer or director should not go beyond it unless the risk in doing so is fully calculated. The history of the theatre is strewn with disasters which could have been averted had those in charge of finance made some attempt to get their sums right and keep within the limits these imposed.

In a professional company, almost every decision in setting up a production will be related to its economics. For that reason there is much to be said for combining the artistic direction with financial administration—always assuming the individual concerned is capable of undertaking both functions. It ensures coherent, co-ordinated planning and prevents misunderstandings, argument and possible recrimination. If responsibility is divided, it is important that there should be the closest possible collaboration in order to arrive at and maintain mutual agreement both on general policy and the budget of each play.

The detailed costing of a production will, of course, vary very much according to circumstances. Rather than discuss the matter hypothetically, it will probably be more helpful to set out the system by which productions at one theatre, the Theatre Royal, Windsor, have been budgeted with reasonable success for many years.

On the income side, the company is entirely self-supporting: it depends upon its box-office takings and the profits from its bars, and as an occasional bonus, a share in the profits of plays to which it has given first production and which have subsequently been presented elsewhere.

The general underlying assumption has always been that the average audience attendance throughout the year will be at least 75 per cent of capacity. This is a much higher figure than is usually adopted—indeed, many companies work on an assumption of no more than 50 per cent capacity. When the Windsor Theatre Company came into being in 1938, two considerations prompted the decision to take a bold rather than cautious course. Since it was strongly held that it is futile to perform to empty seats, it was decided that if the project showed no prospect of building up to an audience of at least three-quarters of capacity, it was not worth continuing. The second consideration was that the higher the standard of production, the more likely it would be to attract an audience. Since production standards are inevitably related to available resources, the bigger the audience, the better the productions—and the bigger the audience. For once, a virtuous circle.

Though there have been many moments of financial crisis, these have almost always been due to rising costs or outside factors rather than to any serious falling-off of audiences, which, through many changes in the price of seats and in the length of run of each play, have held with remarkable consistency to the average attendance figure aimed at. (In recent years it has tended to rise to 80 per cent.)

There is obviously considerable variation between individual productions, some dropping to 60 per cent and others climbing to 98 per cent. In planning the programme, care is taken as far as possible to achieve not only artistic but financial balance as regards both costs and probable earning power. With experience and accumulated knowledge of audience reaction over a period of time, it is possible to guess the latter with reasonable accuracy, although the occasional shock of total miscalculation is a salutory reminder that public taste cannot be taken for granted.

Having decided how much overall is to be spent on a particular production, the first figure to be put down in drawing up the costs is the sum total of overheads, that is, items of expenditure which have to be paid whatever the play. They include such things as rent, rates, staff and orchestra salaries, a proportion based on averages of such things as advertising, telephone and other office expenses, lighting, heating, insurance, audit, pension premiums, maintenance, car maintenance, haulage. An average cost of canvas, wood, paint and other scenery requisites is also included, any expenditure much in excess of this being shown separately. Overheads work out at roughly three-sevenths of capacity.

The costs directly related to the play are 'variables'. They will be governed by the size of the cast, the professional standing and thus salaries of the actors required, the number and nature of costumes needed, the amount of furniture and properties to be procured, whether or not there is a guest director and possibly guest designer (the two often go together), and how much, if anything, is to be paid in royalties to the author; if the production is a musical, further considerations include whether or not the score has to be orchestrated and copied at the company's expense, by how many, if at all, the orchestra has to be augmented, and how many orchestral rehearsals are required.

In London and the Broadway theatre in New York, where actors receive their current market salaries (that is, what their agents expect to be able to get for them), a producer has several factors to consider when assembling his cast. First, how much he can afford overall. Second, what proportion of the total each part is likely to cost, if it is to be well cast. Thirdly, how far a particular actor justifies, both in exceptional suitability for a part and perhaps potential drawing-power, a salary in excess of that figure. Finally, whether to make the necessary adjustments in individual salaries to accommodate such excesses—and thus possibly lower the calibre of the actors in the less important parts—in order to keep within the budget figure, or take a chance that the ideal cast will compensate at the box-office for its extra cost. It is very much a question of judgement, which can only too easily be disastrously wrong.

At Windsor, no serious problem of this sort arises. As with most companies of its kind, it has a 'top' salary which is known to all the artists' agents. It also has a minimum which is somewhat higher than that required by Equity, the actors' union. Thus, the possibility of negotiation is confined—and within narrow limits—to some of the supporting players. It must be added that, as a matter of course, every agent is vehemently convinced that his client, if he has made any kind of professional mark at all and has a part of more then ten lines, is entitled to the 'top' figure. (He is even more likely to try to insist, on the same grounds, that the said client should also be 'billed above the title'—that is that on all publicity matter his name should be printed above the name of the play, a position which commonsense suggests should be reserved for those who would be accepted as 'stars' by the public. In the professional entertainment world the whole question of 'billing' has become a childish game of status, an obsessional 'beat my neighbour', leading to absurd jealousies and bad feeling—and, let it be added, a great many headaches for those who are expected to work out a solution satisfactory to all parties.)

The cast requirement for modern plays seldom exceeds ten. On the other hand, in the less costly days before the second world war, dramatists thought nothing of requiring a cast of fifteen or twenty. With the exception of *Twelfth Night* and *Othello*, no play of Shakespeare can be adequately produced with fewer than twenty-five artists. Against the heavy salary list and the cost of clothing period plays, may be set the fact that their authors have usually died more than fifty years ago and their works are therefore out of copyright or, as it is picturesquely put, 'in the public domain'. Thus no royalty has to be paid upon them.

In the case of plays which are still in copyright, the royalty to be paid may be subject to negotiation, but in the case of amateur productions is usually a flat fee for each performance. Professional companies almost always pay a percentage of the gross box-office receipts (sometimes certain booking-agency discounts having been deducted). This will vary according to circumstances. Although strictly speaking negotiable, it is likely to comply with generally accepted practice; this is that new plays carry a 5 per cent royalty 'all through' when produced by a repertory company or on tour, and in London until a certain figure is reached (nowadays this is usually when the cost of production has been recovered). Thereafter, it will probably be 10 per cent overall.

A production by a repertory company following the London run will carry a royalty of 9 or 10 per cent, of which the author gets two-thirds (less his agent's commission) and the London management the remaining third. When, after some years of insufficient demand, the management ceases to have any rights, the royalty will usually drop to $7\frac{1}{2}$ per cent.

The cost of clothing a production obviously depends very much upon the type of play, the size of the cast and the number of costume changes each actor requires. It is an item which, if it is at all possible, should not be skimped. An audience is likely to be much more conscious—and critical—of the clothes of the actor on whom its eyes are constantly focused than on the scenery, which is, or should be, no more than a background. At Windsor, a permanent wardrobe staff makes all the specially designed costumes for the annual pantomime and musicals, as well as the female costumes for prestige 'open-budgeted' productions of classical revivals. On the whole, however, it is usually found cheaper and more satisfactory to hire 'period' costumes. Modern men's clothes are usually supplied by the actors themselves, a hiring fee being paid to them. Actresses also frequently prefer to provide their own, and are paid a hiring fee. Otherwise their clothes are either made or bought.

The scenery is usually designed by a resident designer, built by a staff consisting of a carpenter and two assistants, and painted by the designer and two assistants. Their salaries are included among the overheads. When a guest designer is brought in, usually by a guest director, not only has his fee to be added to the budget but the probability is that his ideas will be more expansive and costly than the resident designer has become conditioned to accept. Close scrutiny and a liberal contingency fund is advisable on such occasions.

Furniture and properties are usually hired from firms which specialise in this service. Their stocks are extensive, giving reasonable scope for the designer and producer to choose what they want. This goes far towards ensuring a high standard of presentation and is thus well worth the steep hire charges and transportation costs involved.

How much should be spent upon advertising is a matter in which several factors must be taken into account. Its purpose, of course, is to obtain full houses. It is, however, impossible without a referendum to find out why each individual in an audience has decided to attend a particular play. A habit of theatre-going or word-of-mouth recommendation are just as likely reasons as response to paid advertising. It is therefore equally impossible to arrive at a precise optimum figure between over-spending, which may fill the theatre but at the risk of pushing costs beyond possible takings, and under-spending, which may result in insufficient income to cover expenses. At Windsor, the expenditure of approximately 7 per cent of estimated income provides sufficiently wide coverage to maintain satisfactory attendance figures.

How the money is spent has been determined by the fact that the greater part of the Windsor Theatre audience comes from a surrounding district of about twenty-five miles radius. Such a widespread catchment area requires selective rather than saturation publicity methods. For example, to make an effective impression with posters would require much more than their cost would justify. Therefore, only about 250 are used, and at carefully picked key sites such as railway platforms, bus-stops and, of course, outside the theatre itself. Similarly, no more than 500 small 'folio' bills are distributed to pubs, hotels and shops. Valuable though they are, they have a limiting factor. Those who show them usually expect recompense in the form of free seats. If business is, as one hopes, constantly above the 70 per cent mark, this consideration can either be costly or lead to resentment, unless it is made very clear from the outset that the distribution of free seats must be at the management's complete discretion, a matter of privilege rather than right, and will probably be made for performances and plays which are least likely to attract the paying public. In many cases it may reasonably be pointed out that the establishment is, in showing the bill, providing a service for its customers.

One of the most important of the publicity media are the newspapers. A display advertisement, 2in deep across two columns with distinctive type, is inserted in the most widely read local weekly papers in the catchment area. 'Line' advertisements appear in the two local daily papers and in the classified columns of two daily and two Sunday nationals. Most papers give a reasonable coverage in the editorial columns as well as notices by responsible and literate critics.

Probably the most productive method of advertising of all

is direct mail to those who have asked to be informed of the theatre's activities. A card is used, which has the advantage that it requires no envelope, the cost of which and insertion into which is thereby saved; being attractive and distinctive in design, the card's presence among the rest of the mail is unmistakable, and instead of being put unread into the waste-paper basket, it may well find itself on the mantelshelf among the invitation cards. It gives all the relevant information, including a short 'blurb' about the current play and its cast, a one-line mention of the play to follow, and on the reverse side the times of performances and price of seats. Upwards of 10,000 are sent out.

Finally, the Windsor Company publishes an attractive twenty-four-page programme in magazine form, which in addition to articles of general interest and on matters concerning the theatre's policy, gives detailed information about both the current production, with photographs and biographies of all the cast, and the play to follow. It is not only sold in the theatre but widely distributed outside it, especially to valuable vantage places such as doctors' and dentists' waiting-rooms which would not accept straightforward advertising matter. In the long term it has probably contributed more than any other single publicity medium to stimulating and retaining the public's interest in the company and its activities.

Some of the budgeting and advertising methods used at Windsor might well not be suitable for other theatres or drama organisations. Each must work out its own plan, sensibly and thoughtfully based upon its particular circumstances and resources. The all important thing is that there should *be* a plan and that economics are not lost sight of in the heady dreams of splendid artistic endeavour.

POSTSCRIPT

For the most part this book has been written on a note of bright optimism. It has given no hint of the possibility that no play worth producing would be found, that no theatre to present it in would be available, that no money to finance it would be forthcoming, that the producer would not see eye to eye in all things with the director, that the right actors would not be available for all the parts.

In suggesting a schedule for rehearsals it has omitted any mention of its possible dislocation by illness, traffic jams, or the prior claims of film companies on the actors' time. It has described a production period unimpeded by such occurrences as the sets not being ready, the leading lady throwing a temperament because her dresses don't fit, the electric hoist on the house-curtain jamming, the main fuse on the lighting-control board blowing. While admitting that the actors would almost certainly have first-night nerves, it has not visualised any of them breaking an ankle or losing his voice or being incapacitated by mumps. It has discussed the relationship between actor and audience on the rash assumption that there would be an audience.

This idealistic approach was necessary because any other would have opened up a vista of crises of every conceivable kind, a morass in which the purpose of the book—providing a novitiate director with stepping stones to help him on his way—would have become submerged. Yet one must end by saying that it is in his ability to face up to crises, frustrations and disappointments, to overcome or find a way round the unforeseeable snags and hitches which tend to threaten the success of any production, that the director will prove his worth and fitness to survive in a very tough world.

SELECT BIBLIOGRAPHY

Stephen Joseph. *New Theatre Forms*

Stephen Joseph. *Theatre in the Round*

Robert B. Challener. *Play Production Arena Style*

Michael Warre. *Designing and Making Stage Scenery*

David Walker. *Theatrical Set Design. Basic Techniques*

Kenneth Rowell. *Stage Design*

Richard Southern. *Proscenium and Sight-lines*

Thomas Wilfred. *Projected Scenery*

James Laver. *Costume Through The Ages*

Motley. *Designing and Making Stage Costumes*

Frederick Bentham. *The Art of Stage Lighting*

Richard Pilbrow. *Stage Lighting*

H. Hewitt and A. S. Vause. *Lamps and Lighting*

Harold Burris-Meyer and Vincent Mallory. *Sound in the Theatre*

Elizabeth Sweeting. *Theatre Administration*

Hendrik Baker. *Stage Management and Theatrecraft*

APPENDIX I

'CINEMOID COLOUR FILTERS'

Lavender-Gold-Pink

Pale Violet	42	Pink	57
Pale Lavender	36	Middle Rose	10
Gold Tint	51	Dark Pink	11
Pale Gold	52	Deep Salmon	8
Pale Salmon	53	Bright Rose	48
Pale Rose	54	Deep Rose	12
Light Salmon	9	Smoky Pink	27
Light Rose	7	Magenta	13

Yellow-Amber-Red

Pale Yellow	50	Deep Salmon	8
Straw	3	Apricot	47
Yellow	1	Orange	5
Canary	49	Deep Orange	5A
Light Amber	2	Deep Golden Amber	35
Medium Amber	4	Pale Red	66
Chrome Yellow	46	Primary Red	6
Deep Amber	33	Ruby	14
Golden Amber	34		

Blue-Purple-Violet

Turquoise	62	Steel Tint	67
Cyan (Blue-Green)	16	Steel Blue	17
Peacock Blue	15	Daylight	45
Ariel Blue	69	Pale Blue	40

Pale Navy Blue	43	Sky Blue	63
Light Blue	18	Dark Blue	19
Bright Blue	41	Deep Blue	20
Giselle Blue	68	Purple	25
Slate Blue	61	Mauve	26
Medium Blue	32	Pale Violet	42

Green-Neutral-Frost

Pale Green	38	Peacock Blue	15
Pea Green	21	Chocolate Tint	55
Moss Green	22	Pale Chocolate	56
Light Green	23	Pale Grey	60
Dark Green	24	Light Frost	31
Primary Green	39	Heavy Frost	29
Cyan (Blue-Green)	16	Clear	30
Turquoise	62		

APPENDIX II

A PROFESSIONAL COMPANY'S BUDGET

The following tables show, in percentage terms, the proportion of the total expenditure taken by individual items and groups of items in the budget of the Theatre Royal, Windsor. They give a rough idea of 'where the money goes' in an English professional company, producing plays of every kind for three-weekly runs.

The first table relates to one year's trading and includes both 'overheads' and 'variables' (see pages 121–2). The second table gives the 'variables' only of four different types of production. The degree of variation depends upon both the nature and the scale of each play and its consequent total cost. The difference in costs between the examples given would, very approximately, be:

$$A = \pounds x, \quad B = \pounds x + \frac{x}{4}, \quad C = \pounds x + \frac{x}{2}, \quad \text{and of } D = \pounds x + \frac{3x}{4}.$$

TABLE 1: COSTS OF ONE YEAR'S TRADING

Salaries	%
Actors	21·82
carry forward	21·82

Salaries %

brought forward 21·82

Orchestra 6·82
    Musical Director
    5 Instrumentalists

Stage Management and Stage Staff 17·58
    Associate Producer
    Production Manager
    Head of Design
    2 Assistant Scenic Artists
    Head Carpenter
    2 Assistant Carpenters
    Electrician
    Assistant Electrician
    Head of Wardrobe
    2 Assistants
    2 Stage Managers
    2 Assistant Stage Managers
    Dayman
    Fireman
    Telephonist

Administration 7·57
    Managing Director
    Deputy Managing Director
    Business Manager
    Assistant Manager
    Secretary
    Publicity Manager
    Assistant Publicity Manager
    Auditor

carry forward 53·79

Salaries	%
brought forward	53·79
Front of House	5·06
Box-Office Manager	
3 Box-Office Assistants	
Linkman	
6 Cleaners	
6 Ushers	
National Health Insurance	1·90
Staff Pension Scheme	1·48
Production Expenses (less salaries)	12·46
Rent and Rates	2·48
Light and Heat	2·00
Telephone and Cables	·70
Insurance	1·09
Car Expenses	·31
Travelling	·05
Entertainment	·44
Repairs to Premises	1·16
Repairs and Replacements—Fixtures	1·27
Advertising, Printing and Stationery	7·63
Cleaning	·61
Royalties	5·75
Sundry Trade Expenses	·64
Subscriptions and Donations	·15
Legal Expenses	·03
Depreciation	1·00
	100·00

TABLE 2: 'VARIABLES' FOR FOUR DIFFERENT EXAMPLES OF PRODUCTIONS

	A *Revival of a modern play with 4 actors and 1 set*	B *New modern play with 10 actors and 2 sets*	C *Shakespearian play with 25 actors*	D *Revival of a modern costume play with 25 actors*
	%	%	%	%
Actors, including proportion of rehearsal salaries	44·08	57·00	69·80	59·42
Extra Stage Hands for 'set-up'	4·20	4·20	2·42	2·06
National Health Insurance	7·89	5·20	3·49	2·97
Author's Royalty	7½ of takings	5 of takings		10 of takings
	29·60	12·40	0·00	12·40
Hire Charges				
Furniture and Props	7·89	10·00	2·81	2·48
Costumes	0·00	0·00	14·56	12·40
Extra Lighting	0·00	0·00	0·97	2·48
Purchases Costumes Costume Materials Properties First Night Flowers Food for Dress-Rehearsal	6·34	11·20	5·95	5·79

INDEX